Building
BRIDGES

A Thematic Approach to College Reading & Writing

Department of English
New York City College of Technology
City University of New York

Anna H.-J. Do

Kendall Hunt
publishing company

Cover images © Shutterstock, Inc.

Kendall Hunt
publishing company

www.kendallhunt.com
Send all inquiries to:
4050 Westmark Drive
Dubuque, IA 52004-1840

Copyright © 2013 by Kendall Hunt Publishing Company

ISBN 978-1-4652-1539-0

Printed in the United States of America
10 9 8 7 6 5 4 3

To my mother and father,
who gave me my love of language.

contents

UNIT 2: Home and Family   37

Chapter 3: My Two Lives 39

Chapter 4: Life's Travels for a Father and a Son 57

UNIT 3: People and Society 79

UNIT 4: Food and Health　　　　　　　　　125

UNIT 6: Technology   225

UNIT 7: Moving Forward   265

Chapter 13: Making Waves at the Seaport......................................*267*

Chapter 14: After 20 Years, Is the Website about to Become Extinct? 287

foreword

An ancient Chinese philosopher cautioned us that "Every journey must begin with a first step." Dr. Anna H.-J. Do deserves our gratitude for her well researched text, *Building Bridges* that builds the foundation of "first steps."

While all undergraduate English students will benefit from her smartly constructed 14-chapter text, addressing 21st century issues ranging from "Home and Family" to "Technology," I suspect struggling learners and ESL students will find her prereading, vocabulary in context, and postreading strategies particularly useful. Each of the chapter topics uses current excerpts from popular journals and publications. Students then develop their reading and writing expertise through a rich fabric of research-based assessments and class discussions that invite them to drill down to critical reading, analytic and inferential skills. Each chapter then concludes with extensive writing and application challenges to ensure learning.

Dr. Do's textbook not only guides students to take their first undergraduate steps in language comprehension but as importantly, it ensures that they have learned the essential lessons for their journey of lifelong learning.

Ronald D. Valenti, Ph.D.
Director
Ed. D. Program in Executive Leadership
The College of New Rochelle
Westchester County, NY
June 2011

preface

Building Bridges, a theme-centered text, provides a complete process of research-based instruction that fully integrates reading and writing. This volume follows the prereading, during-reading, and postreading strategies that many scholars and practitioners have advocated and proven to be an effective reading/teaching tool. This book also offers comprehensive exercises for vocabulary words, which is essential for improving reading comprehension. Articles are drawn from local newspapers and magazines which build the connection from the readers' cultural experiences to texts, providing a reading/writing scaffold to stabilize the students' fundamental skills whereby they become self-supporting in college.

FEATURES OF BUILDING BRIDGES

Prereading

Prereading assists the student to interact with the reading material creating a richer, more stimulating experience, which will be applied throughout each chapter. It intends to tap students' prior knowledge and experiences as they relate to the theme of the chapter and create visual pictures to support better understanding of reading.

Vocabulary in Context

The goal of this section is to familiarize the student with speaking and thinking in a way that may not be comfortable for them at first but gives a cerebral challenge. This section allows students to identify the part of speech and to guess the meaning of the word using context clues.

The Reading Process

This section outlines/covers topics, main ideas, details of each reading, open-ended questions, relating to yourself, drawing inferences, useful words/phrases, idiomatic expressions, and vocabulary practice. The students may ruminate on the passage rather than gloss over them so they can broaden their reading comprehension by analyzing each reading in-depth.

Postreading

This portion of *Building Bridges* addresses how the reader can make connections from reading to writing. It beckons the reader to a written response based on their reaction to the reading passage. Postreading invites the reader to reflect on their relationship to what they have just read through the metacognitive process.

Writing a Summary

The students are expected to utilize their writing abilities based on the given outline to communicate the understanding of the reading text. Summarizing a text is a valuable way to check the understanding of the text, which is also a precursor facilitating the students to think clearly and write logically.

Application

Application is at the core of every instructor's desire for the learner to be able to draw conclusions and integrate what they have learned. The Internet has opened up the floodgate to all students. Instructors expect their college students to have a working relationship with the Internet to expand the classroom, taking their coursework to the next level. Internet activities pose questions about the text that students must answer using links provided, e-portfolio, and Blackboard for posting discussions.

Reading-response journal acts as a writing prompt to allow the student to construct a brief essay related to the theme which was focused on in the text. Journal writing helps students to process information from the text to develop their awareness. It is a thought processing tool used to develop written self-expression.

Building Critical Thinking

This section begins in Chapter 5 and culminates in Chapter 14. Each chapter asks students to develop an outline consisting of an introductory paragraph, three body paragraphs, and a concluding paragraph. This process creates thought organization in college level writing. It is a visual structure designed to give the writer parameters for their composition. Its framework connects students' ideas from the text to their real-life experience.

Grammar Practice via Internet

This section presents links to websites where the user can interface with online services. Each website is designed for the student to research grammar components that are related to the reading text.

Building Bridges is a working text with consideration for the 21st century's college students and instructors. The text is formatted in an easy-to-read style, visual allure, current themes and topics, and thought-provoking questions to enhance reading and writing habits through the use of Internet and online activities, whereby each student realizes their potential for success on their academic journey.

ACKNOWLEDGEMENT

Completing this book has been a long and challenging journey of logical thought and careful writing. My sincerest appreciation goes to the members of the project team, Sarah Flynn and Sue Saad, and of the permissions team, Tammy Hunt, at Kendall Hunt for their support throughout the project. Special thanks goes to the Project Coordinator, Sara McGovern, for facilitating the updated edition. I'm especially grateful to my developmental editor, Annette Rivera, for her diligent work and invaluable suggestions during the preparation of this volume. My colleagues and students deserve more than a mere acknowledgement. Many thanks to Monique Ferrell for encouraging me to write a textbook. I also thank Barbara Guinan, Grazyna Kenda, Beverly Marshack, and Roland Valenti for offering helpful materials and valuable suggestions during the preparation of this edition of Building Bridges. My students have always been a driving force for me to strive to be a teacher of excellence. I thank them for their support and agreement to use their writings and pictures to be included in this volume. I'm particularly indebted to Dr. Roland Valenti, Director of the Ed. D. program in Executive Leadership at the College of New Rochelle, New York, for writing a Foreword to this book. My special thanks to my precious children, Juno and Hannah, for giving me joy and happiness during this arduous task.

Anna H.-J. Do
Brooklyn, New York
November, 2012

Image © blinkblink, 2012, Shutterstock, Inc.

unit 1

STARTING OUT

chapter 1

BREAKING GROUND

Your Goals in Mind

Write what you think reading and writing are about and what you desire to accomplish by studying this book.

_____

_____

_____

_____

_____

_____

_____

_____

_____

_____

_____

_____

_____

The Reading Process

What Is Reading?

Reading is a process of constructing meaning by interacting with text; as individuals read, they use their prior knowledge along with clues from the text to construct meaning. Research indicates that effective or expert readers are strategic (Baker & Brown, 1984).[1]

Reading is a means of language acquisition, of communication, and of sharing information and ideas. Like all language, it is a complex interaction between the text and the reader that is shaped by the reader's prior knowledge, experiences, attitude, and language community which is culturally and socially situated. The reading process requires continuous practice, development, and refinement. **http://en.wikipedia.org/wiki/Reading_(process)**

Reading Strategies

Step 1: Prereading

This stage places a great emphasis on the importance of activating the reader's background knowledge to relate to the text. Pictures trigger the reader's imagination to connect personal experiences with the reading text.

Step 2: During reading

Vocabulary skills, figurative language, and thought-provoking questions assist the reader to comprehend passages. The metacognitive process asks the reader to analyze the motive of the author.

Step 3: Postreading

The final reading strategy assesses students' comprehension of the reading material, as it relates to their point of reference.

---

1. Baker, L. & Brown, A.L. (1984). Metacognitive skills and reading. In P.D. Pearson (Ed.), *Handbook of reading research* (pp. 353–394). New York: Longman.

THE WRITING PROCESS

1. In Your Own Words: Introduce Yourself

Write a two-paragraph essay about yourself. One should address aspects of your personal life, such as family and the other, academic experiences in school or social life.

Read some of your peers' testimonies before writing your own on the lines provided.

Image © SVLuma, 2012. Shutterstock, Inc.

Student 1

"I'm a very nice outgoing person. I'm always smiling and laughing. My life is full of positive outcomes. I'm very glad I came so far to attend college. I made my family proud and also myself.

"I'm a family person. Everything I do is for my family. I want to become a more knowledgeable person to have many opportunities in life. I want to have a good career and have a family of my own one day. Last but not least, I thank God for everything and He always came first in my life."

—Tiffany Pagan

Student 2

"It's not much to say about me but I'm a happy all the time fun girl. I love food and cooking. I also like being around my friends and family. I was very close to my uncle until he passed away. Now I'm close to my little cousin. We have a lot of fun together and I love her a lot.

"I also like to dance around my house and play video games with my mother. She loves video games more than anything and sometimes we watch movies together. My father and I love to shop a lot. That's mostly what we do together. I have two dogs and a cat. My dogs' names are Chicko and Diesel, and my cat's name is Pebbles. I have many friends and we like to go out and have fun all the time together. I'm not too much of a person who likes school but I still try my hardest."

—Jasmine Temple

Student 3

"My name is Fatoumata Toure. As you can see that's an African name. Both my parents are from West Africa, Mali and I was born and raised here in the U.S.A. This is my first year of College and I'm planning on finishing college with a business degree.

"I've visited Mali once and I loved it. Being around my family that I never knew I had was amazing. I only live in the U.S.A. with my Mom, Dad, and younger brother. I am planning on finishing my education here at City Tech and succeed with my dreams of being in business management."

—Fatoumata Toure

2. In Your Own Words: How to Become a Better Student

Write what you can do to become a better student.

Read some of your peers' testimonies before writing your own on the lines provided.

Student 1

"Improvement and adjustment to a new learning environment can sometimes be difficult but both have the same basic fundamentals, hard work and dedication. To be the best pupil you can be, one must be open-minded and willing to learn unconditionally. Personally, as it is my first year attending college these truths hold tremendous weight as I step onto a higher ladder of education. To dismiss and overcome obstacles that stand in one's path is also part of the recipe of success. From disruptive students to personal external issues, one has to overcome and persevere to achieve one's goals. One simple way I can ensure my success and be a better student is to be on time as so much of being successful derives from attending your courses punctually and attentively."

—Dionel Then

Student 2

"In order to become a productive student, taking steps such as gaining confidence and comfort around unfamiliar faces can illustrate how well a person can use communication to their advantage. Through experience comes wisdom, therefore those bad decisions we once made during high school in and out of class shouldn't be reiterated. Picking up on bad habits like leaving assignments for last minute or going to a party instead of studying for a big exam, are just few of many examples of how one has the ability to change for the better. The race against time is never-ending, and that is why managing it is in my opinion the best way to succeed in school. Knowing when things are due, understanding what a teacher is explaining, and asking questions are three simple approaches to overcoming any doubts or concerns a person may be dealing with. Easier said than done, but with some effort nearly everything can be accomplished."

—Kenny Matute

Process of Writing

- **Prewriting** is brainstorming. Brainstorming is a tool writers use to jot down thoughts which come into the mind spontaneously.

- **Drafting.** The writer creates an outline based on ideas generated during brainstorming.

- **Revising.** A written material encourages the student to take ownership of their writing, molding it into a presentable masterpiece.

- **Editing** fine-tunes your written work by repairing grammar, spelling, punctuation, and capitalization.

Practice Makes Perfect!

Practice 1

Read the paragraph below and answer the questions that follow.

Paragraph is a group of sentences that develops a main idea. A well-written paragraph should be coherent, unified, and fully developed, and indented for academic writing.

Of the four problems, the most serious environmental concern, in my judgment, is polluted air. In evaluating air pollution, the scientific conclusion is that it is a very serious health hazard. Carbon dioxide and pollutants are known to cause lung, respiratory, and related physical problems. Three specific actions I would take to correct air pollution are (1) pass legislation that would restrict the number of cars, buses, and trucks allowed in the city during working hours; (2) require that all vehicles must have catalytic converters to reduce carbon dioxide emissions; and (3) require all manufacturers and factories with CO_2 emissions to take the necessary steps to reduce pollutant emissions. In summation, it is to our advantage that we consider improved ways to interact with our environment.

1. Formulate your title for this reading.

_____

Formulating the Right Title

- Develop a title that attracts the reader's attention.
- The right title gives the reader an idea of what the passage is about.
- Your title plays a role in connecting to the main idea of the passage.

2. What is the topic, or subject of this reading? Use the fewest words possible.

_____

_____

Topic is the subject of a paragraph. It is what a paragraph is about.

3. What is the main idea of this text? Underline it if directly stated. Write it in your own words if implied.

_____

_____

Topic sentence is the main idea of a paragraph. A well-written paragraph should have a sentence that clearly states the main idea of the paragraph, which is also called the *topic sentence*. A good topic sentence consists of a topic and the author's point of view or idea on the topic. This idea controls the author's choice of details, which is called the *controlling idea*. A topic sentence usually appears at the beginning of a paragraph but can also appear in the middle or at the end. For some paragraphs, a main idea or topic sentence is not clearly stated, but implied or suggested. In such cases, you have to figure out implied main ideas through supporting details.

4. How is the main idea supported in the passage?

_____

_____

_____

Supporting details consist of examples, facts, reasons, statistics, quotations, or personal experiences to support the main idea. A good writer must provide sufficient details enabling the reader to establish missing information that will help convey the thoughts and ideas of the writer.

Now that you've completed reading comprehension questions, we are moving toward writing. The passage you just read is indeed a model paragraph written based on the essay topic below.

WRITE *YOUR* PARAGRAPH NOW! The model paragraph should give you some ideas as to how to write your own.

ONE-PARAGRAPH WRITING Suppose you're given a financial grant to correct only one of these three environmental problems: (1) lack of parks and recreational areas; (2) littered streets; and (3) excessive traffic. Select one environmental problem and write a paragraph that responds to each of the three questions below.

1. Which of these three problems would you correct with your financial grant?

2. Why did you select this specific problem to correct?

3. Identify three steps/actions you would take a correct this problem.

_____

_____

_____

_____

_____

_____

_____

_____

_____

_____

_____

_____

_____

_____

_____

Practice 2

Read the following longer essay and answer the questions that follow.

[1]   My 15-year-old son lies on the couch half awake ignoring the snooze button once again for the tenth time in the past half-hour. What is it that makes one immune to a throbbing beep to claim nine more minutes of shut-eye? Who knows! Then all at once it happens. He arises from the sunken cushion and taps the screen stopping the infernal pong. Now the dance begins. "Where are you going?" I say. Annoyed he responds, "Out!" By now you're saying, where is the next rung in this ladder in understanding the meaning of love. It is a simple seven letter word called F-R-E-E-D-O-M. It is the cry of every human soul. Love is just that simple. It is in one's ability to be free. Freedom to choose, to be, to come and go, and grow and change, to hurt and heal and to make mistakes and learn from them.

[2]   Turn the clock back to 1990 and now my story begins. I had just found faith and was looking for a ministry where I could plug in to and show my new-found people skills. Then one day it found me. A prison pen pal ministry. It was perfect. I could write a few letters, and send a picture, a gift at Christmas. Yes, it was just the kind of Polly-Anna pen pal I could wrap my life around. A long distance commitment with a hint of caring. However, when you get God involved, it never is a small event. He has a picture that is larger than life.

[3]   My incarcerated friend was called Elle. Elle might have been born on another planet for all I knew. Our common thread which we used to create the masterpiece of a two-year relationship was our faith. She had struggles which left her divorced at a young age, a runaway from an abusive family system, and dependent on a man who allowed her to take the rap being charged with Grand Larceny. For two years we wrote letters every week. I sent slippers and stamps. I became my friend's anchor to the outside world. I visited her at the Women's Correctional Facility where we first met. We had a photo taken. I went home to tell of the wonderful story of the way I was being used to help a poor misguided women turn around her life. Little did I realize, Elle was teaching me the greater lesson. It was the Spring of 1992 when Elle wrote and said she would be getting out. She would transition to a half-way house down in South Jersey. We had agreed to meet and spend the day celebrating her "new found freedom." As I drove down the shore for

three hours my head whirred with anticipation. I was filled with excitement and a strange fear that something was ending as well as beginning.

[4]   I arrived at her house and waited patiently in the kitchen staring blankly at a wall calendar, when all of a sudden I was charged with an embrace that almost snapped my neck. My friend Elle's hug was the hug of life, I will never forget that scene or embrace as I never felt it again. It was here that I understood what true love meant. It was sacrifice, service, selfless giving, struggle, and most of all, it was the passion of a soul set free.

[5]   The rest of that afternoon we spent eating out on the boardwalk at a fancy restaurant, going on a roller coaster which was a once-in-a-lifetime event even for me, and catching up on new plans for Elle's future. Love is a mysterious thing but never is it stagnant, it grows and dies and resurrects itself in new forms over and over. The trick is to be able to get a glimpse of love's many practical sides and be willing to embrace it with open arms.

—Annette Rivera

1. Formulate your title for this reading.

   _____

2. What is the topic, or subject of this reading? Use the fewest words possible.

   _____

3. What is the main idea of this text? Underline it if directly stated. Write it in your own words if implied.

   _____

   _____

Thesis Statement is the main idea of an entire passage that involves more than one paragraph. It should contain the topic of the passage and author's point of view on the topic.

4. How is the main idea supported in the essay?

_____

_____

_____

5. Why is the long distance relationship appealing/unappealing to many people?

_____

_____

_____

ONE-PARAGRAPH WRITING Can you describe a time where you extended your friendship to someone with the purpose of getting nothing in return? Formulate a title for this topic in using only four words. Based on the *Study Notes* below, develop a one-paragraph argumentative essay with a main idea and two supporting details.

_____

_____

_____

_____

Study Notes – Descriptive Writing

INSPIRATION

- The purpose of a descriptive essay is to describe events, people, and places.

- Descriptive writing uses sensory details to picture what you are writing about. Be sure to include sufficient vivid details.

- The details of the controlling idea should be arranged in spatial organization or some other logical format.

APPLICATION

Internet Activities

1. Do you have a career goal? Have you met with a career counselor to explore possible careers? Check out your college's website and click on career services or counseling to find out what services are available for you.

_____

_____

_____

_____

_____

2. Pull up your college's website and check out job opportunities. Bring in job ads that appeal to you and compare them with your classmates.

GRAMMAR PRACTICE VIA INTERNET

Go to one of the following websites:

- http://www.englishclub.com/grammar/parts-of-speech_1.htm

- http://www.writingcentre.uottawa.ca/hypergrammar/partsp.html

Research the parts of speech and write the definition for each part of speech on the lines provided. Choose any sentence in the passage in Chapter 1 and write the parts of speech.

_____

_____

_____

_____

_____

_____

_____

_____

_____

_____

_____

_____

chapter 2
STUDENT EXPECTATIONS SEEN AS CAUSING GRADE DISPUTES

PREREADING

Class Discussion

Discuss the following questions in a group.

1. What do you do to earn an A in your classes?

   _____

   _____

2. What do the pictures on the next page remind you of?

   _____

   _____

3. Predict what the text will be about by reading the title.

   _____

   _____

4. Predict what the text will be about by reading the first and last paragraphs (See pages 22-24).

   _____

   _____

Image © Vixit, 2012. Shutterstock, Inc.

Professor Ellen Greenberger studied what she found to be an increased sense of entitlement among college students.

5. Write how the author would develop the story.

_____

_____

Vocabulary in Context

Each item below includes a sentence from the reading. Using the context clues from this sentence, (1) determine the part of speech, and (2) formulate your own definition for the underlined word. Then (3) locate the word in a dictionary and write the appropriate definition.

Image © Andresr, 2012. Shutterstock, Inc.

1. "Many students come in with the <u>conviction</u> that they've worked hard and deserve a higher mark." (Paragraph 2)

(1) _____

(2) _____

(3) _____

2. "Professor Greenberger said that the sense of <u>entitlement</u> could be related to increased parental pressure, competition among peers and family members, and a heightened sense of achievement anxiety." (7)

(1) _____

(2) _____

(3) _____

3. "I think that it <u>stems</u> from their K-12 experiences." (9)

(1) _____

(2) _____

(3) _____

4. "I think putting in a lot of effort should <u>merit</u> a high grade." (13)

(1) _____

(2) _____

(3) _____

5. "Dean Hogge said, "Professors often try to outline the 'rules of the game' in their syllabi," in an effort to <u>curb</u> haggling over grades." (18)

(1) _____

(2) _____

(3) _____

6. "Dean Hogge said, "Professors often try to outline the 'rules of the game' in their syllabi," in an effort to curb <u>haggling</u> over grades." (18)

   (1) _____

   (2) _____

   (3) _____

7. "He said that if students developed a genuine interest in their field, grades would take a back seat, and <u>holistic</u> and intrinsically motivated learning could take place." (23)

   (1) _____

   (2) _____

   (3) _____

8. "He said that if students developed a genuine interest in their field, grades would take a back seat, and holistic and <u>intrinsically</u> motivated learning could take place." (23)

   (1) _____

   (2) _____

   (3) _____

READING
. . . .

STUDENT EXPECTATIONS SEEN AS CAUSING GRADE DISPUTES

— Max Roosevelt

[1]   Prof. Marshall Grossman has come to expect complaints whenever he returns graded papers in his English classes at the University of Maryland.

[2]   "Many students come in with the conviction that they've worked hard and

deserve a higher mark," Professor Grossman said. "Some assert that they have never gotten a grade as low as this before."

[3]   He attributes those complaints to his students' sense of entitlement.

[4]   "I tell my classes that if they just do what they are supposed to do and meet the standard requirements, that they will earn a C," he said. "That is the default grade. They see the default grade as an A."

[5]   A recent study by researchers at the University of California, Irvine, found that a third of students surveyed said that they expected B's just for attending lectures, and 40 percent said they deserved a B for completing the required reading.

[6]   "I noticed an increased sense of entitlement in my students and wanted to discover what was causing it," said Ellen Greenberger, the lead author of the study, called "Self-Entitled College Students: Contributions of Personality, Parenting, and Motivational Factors," which appeared last year in *The Journal of Youth and Adolescence*.

[7]   Professor Greenberger said that the sense of entitlement could be related to increased parental pressure, competition among peers and family members, and a heightened sense of achievement anxiety.

[8]   Aaron M. Brower, the vice provost for teaching and learning at the University of Wisconsin-Madison, offered another theory.

[9]   "I think that it stems from their K-12 experiences," Professor Brower said. "They have become ultra-efficient in test preparation. And this hyper-efficiency has led them to look for a magic formula to get high scores."

[10]   James Hogge, associate dean of the Peabody School of Education at Vanderbilt University, said: "Students often confuse the level of effort with the quality of work. There is a mentality in students that 'if I work hard, I deserve a high grade.' "

[11]   In line with Dean Hogge's observation are Professor Greenberger's test results. Nearly two-thirds of the students surveyed said that if they explained to a professor that they were trying hard, that should be taken into account in their grade.

[12]   Jason Greenwood, a senior kinesiology major at the University of Maryland echoed that view.

[13]   "I think putting in a lot of effort should merit a high grade," Mr. Greenwood said. "What else is there really than the effort that you put in?"

[14]   "If you put in all the effort you have and get a C, what is the point?" he added. "If someone goes to every class and reads every chapter in the book and does everything the teacher asks of them and more, then they should be getting an A like their effort deserves. If your maximum effort can only be average in a teacher's mind, then something is wrong."

[15]   Sarah Kinn, a junior English major at the University of Vermont, agreed, saying, "I feel that if I do all of the readings and attend class regularly, that I should be able to achieve a grade of at least a B."

[16]   At Vanderbilt, there is an emphasis on what Dean Hogge calls "the locus of control." The goal is to put the academic burden on the student.

[17]   "Instead of getting an A, they make an A," he said. "Similarly, if they make a lesser grade, it is not the teacher's fault. Attributing the outcome of a failure to someone else is a common problem."

[18]   Additionally, Dean Hogge said, "professors often try to outline the 'rules of the game' in their syllabi," in an effort to curb haggling over grades.

[19]   Professor Brower said professors at Wisconsin emphasized that students must "read for knowledge and write with the goal of exploring ideas."

[20]   This informal mission statement, along with special seminars for freshmen, is intended to help "re-teach students about what education is."

[21]   The seminars are integrated into introductory courses. Examples include the conventional, like a global-warming seminar, and the more obscure, like physics in religion.

[22]   The seminars "are meant to help students think differently about their classes and connect them to real life," Professor Brower said.

[23]   He said that if students developed a genuine interest in their field, grades would take a back seat, and holistic and intrinsically motivated learning could take place.

[24]   "College students want to be part of a different and better world, but they don't know how," he said. "Unless teachers are very intentional with our goals, we play into the system in place."

THE READING PROCESS

Topics, Main Ideas, and Details

1. What is the topic, or subject of this reading? Use the fewest words possible.

   _____

2. What is the main idea of this text? Underline it if directly stated. Write it in your own words if implied.

   _____

   _____

3. How is the main idea supported in the passage?

   _____

   _____

Identifying Details

Answer the following questions in complete sentences.

1. Why do college students feel entitled to A's and B's?

   _____

   _____

   _____

2. What grade will students receive for doing only the requirements and why?

   _____

   _____

   _____

3. What do professors do in order to curb haggling over students' grades?

_____

_____

_____

4. According to Professor Brower, what should motivate students?

_____

_____

_____

5. What is the purpose of the seminars that are integrated into introductory courses?

_____

_____

_____

Relate to Yourself

Answer the following questions in complete sentences.

1. Do you believe you deserve a high grade if you work hard, regardless of the quality of your work? Explain why.

_____

_____

_____

2. What do you suggest you need to do to become a successful student? List your suggestions.

_____

_____

CHAPTER 2: Student Expectations Seen as Causing Grade Disputes

Drawing Inferences

The following information is not directly stated in the reading. Indicate whether the statement is true or false by writing T or F in the spaces provided.

_____ 1. The default grade is an A.

_____ 2. Students are convinced that hard work equals a high grade.

_____ 3. Parents are unconcerned about their children's grades.

_____ 4. Instructors attempt to motivate their students in the hope of developing a love of learning.

Useful Words/Phrases

1. In Paragraph 17, the author uses a word *similarly*. What are the words or phrases that can replace the word *similarly*? How do they function in sentences?

   _____

   _____

2. In Paragraph 18, the author uses a word *additionally*. What are the words or phrases that can replace the word *additionally*? How do they function in sentences?

   _____

   _____

3. In Paragraph 20, the author uses a phrase *along with*. What are the words or phrases that can replace the phrase *along with*? How do they function in sentences?

   _____

   _____

Idiomatic Expressions

1. In Paragraph 16, what is meant by *locus of control*?

   _____

2. In Paragraph 23, what does it mean by *take a back seat*?

   _____

Vocabulary Practice

Match the underlined words with their definitions in the box. Write the appropriate answer letter in the spaces provided.

_____ 1. I <u>attribute</u> my success to hard work.

_____ 2. A dog's <u>heightened</u> sense of smell can even sniff out cancer.

_____ 3. His misbehavior <u>stems</u> from his lack of discipline at home.

_____ 4. Many children do not understand that playing with friends is a privilege, not an <u>entitlement.</u>

_____ 5. When the young boy over-reacted, he was told to <u>curb</u> his enthusiasm.

_____ 6. Since the opposing team didn't have enough players, we won by <u>default.</u>

_____ 7. Due to his unwavering <u>conviction</u> of justice, the police officer often went the extra mile to catch criminals.

_____ 8. The painting <u>echoed</u> the beautiful countryside of Italy.

_____ 9. That comment did not <u>merit</u> such a venomous response.

_____ 10. The <u>locus</u> of modern science was Italy during the Renaissance Era.

_____ 11. The man was so miserly that he was constantly <u>haggling</u> with merchants for a better price.

_____ 12. The manager ingeniously <u>integrated</u> the new policies into the new training program.

_____ 13. His <u>genuine</u> eagerness to help was a bit annoying at times.

_____ 14. <u>Holistic</u> medicine treats both the body and mind.

_____ 15. Once he found a field he enjoyed, he was able to stay <u>intrinsically</u> motivated.

a. belief that one is deserving of privileges or rewards

b. a strong persuasion or belief

c. originates/starts/comes from

d. real/sincere

e. to regard as resulting from a specified cause

f. a selection that is made automatically or without active consideration

g. concerned with complete systems rather than the analysis of individual parts

h. something that has become greater compared to usual standards

i. to put a boundary around something

j. argue to get your way

k. to make a part of something

l. doing something without an outside stimuli

m. origination; beginning; at the very center

n. repeat or imitate

o. earn

POSTREADING

Reading Strategies

Read the questions below and answer in the spaces provided.

1. In reading this passage, what are you reminded of?

    Answer: This reading reminds me of _____

    _____

2. Were you satisfied with your prereading prediction about the text?

    Answer: I was/wasn't satisfied because _____

    _____

3. Do you have any questions about the reading?

    Answer: I wonder _____

    _____

4. What did you visualize while reading this passage?

    Answer: I visualized _____

    _____

5. Is this passage making sense to you?

    Answer: This passage is/isn't making sense to me because _____

    _____

6. What is the main idea of this reading?

    Answer: This reading is about _____

    _____

7. How can you relate the main idea to your own experiences?

   Answer: I can relate this passage to _____

   _____

8. Comment on the author's style of writing.

   Answer: When I read this passage, I feel _____

   _____

9. What have you learned?

   Answer: I have learned _____

   _____

10. During your reading of the text, what appeals to you that you'd like to try in your own writing?

    Answer: In my next writing I will try _____

    _____

Study Notes: Developing a Summary Paragraph

A summary is a condensed version of a larger reading passage. It briefly presents in your own words the main ideas and relevant details of the piece you've read. A summary is not to rewrite but to communicate basic ideas to the readers. Therefore, writing a good summary requires your clear understanding of the reading.

INSPIRATION

Your one-paragraph summary should include:

(1) The full name of the author

(2) The title of the piece, in quotation marks

(3) Source and date of the piece

(4) The main thesis

(5) Two or three supporting ideas the writer uses to develop the thesis

Note:

(1) Keep who, what, when, where, why, and how questions in mind.

(2) You may include quotations, but most of the writing should be in your own words.

(3) Do not include your opinion or response to the reading.

Study Notes: Three Easy Steps in Writing a Summary

Step 1: Start with an introductory sentence that presents the main part of the piece you've read and explain the author's purpose in writing the article.

INSPIRATION

Step 2: Provide specific information about the author's purpose and main point, and include specific examples so that the reader can appreciate the value of the author's message.

Step 3: Finish with a concluding sentence that summarizes the author's main point.

Practice Makes Perfect!

Summarize the reading passage in one paragraph, by following the aforementioned instructions.

GUIDED SUMMARY Begin writing a summary by completing the sentence below.

In "Student Expectations Seen as Causing Grade Disputes" (*New York Times*, 2009), author Max Roosevelt shows that

_____

_____

_____

_____

_____

_____

_____

_____

_____

_____

_____

_____

_____

_____

_____

_____

APPLICATION

Internet Activities

1. Using any search engine, locate Professor Brower at Wisconsin. Which department is he in? What is his title? Can you find his areas of expertise?

   _____

   _____

2. Search your college's website for the student handbook. What are the college's expectations for obtaining high grades?

   _____

   _____

3. Check if your college website offers e-portfolios. Create your account and get ready to post your pieces of writing. Post your discussion to Blackboard as a class discussion.

Reading-response Journal

1. Which of the two, do you think should reflect your grades, effort or achievement? Explain why.

   _____

   _____

   _____

   _____

   _____

   _____

   _____

   _____

2. Some people say that American college professors should not count "class participation" as part of a grade since immigrant students are generally more hesitant to speak up in class than are American-born students. These people claim that the class participation grade is discriminatory and unfair toward immigrant students. However, there are those who would argue that one of the best ways to learn in our classrooms is to ask questions and to speak up on a regular basis.

Which view would you argue for? Based on the *Study Notes* below, develop a one-paragraph argumentative essay with a main idea and two supporting details.

_____

_____

_____

_____

_____

_____

_____

_____

Study Notes: Argumentative Essay

INSPIRATION

- The purpose of an argumentative essay is to convince the reader to agree with your point of view.

- The argumentative essay needs to be logical and persuasive by providing sufficient supporting details and explaining the reasons.

- Supporting materials can consist of facts, examples, scientific data, statistics, and experts' opinions.

- Refuting the opposing argument can enhance your own points.

GRAMMAR PRACTICE VIA INTERNET

Go to one of the following websites:

- http://www.englishpage.com/verbpage/verbtenseintro.html

- http://leo.stcloudstate.edu/grammar/tenses.html

- http://owl.english.purdue.edu/owl/resource/601/01/

Research these tenses on the Internet: *simple present*, *present progressive*, and *present perfect*. Write the definition for each on the lines provided.

Identify a sentence for each tense in the reading. Write the verb and discuss its function on the lines below.

_____

_____

_____

_____

_____

_____

_____

_____

_____

_____

_____

_____

unit 2

HOME AND FAMILY

chapter 3

MY TWO LIVES

PREREADING

Class Discussion

Discuss the following questions in a group.

1. Have you ever travelled to another country? If so, name one thing that was different from the one in your country.

   _____

   _____

   _____

2. What do the pictures on the next page remind you of?

   _____

   _____

   _____

3. Predict what the text will be about by reading the title.

   _____

   _____

   _____

Not an ice skater: A bicultural upbringing is a rich but imperfect thing.

Image © Nitr, 2012. Shutterstock, Inc.

Image © Joe Gough, 2012. Shutterstock, Inc.

"Around non-Indian friends, I no longer feel compelled to hide the fact that I speak another language. I speak Bengali to my children."

4. Predict what the text will be about by reading the first and last paragraphs (See pages 43-45).

    _____

    _____

5. Write how the author would develop the story.

    _____

    _____

Vocabulary in Context

Each item below includes a sentence from the reading. Using the context clues from this sentence, (1) determine the part of speech, and (2) formulate your own definition for the underlined word. Then (3) locate the word in a dictionary and write the appropriate definition.

1. "Like many immigrant <u>offspring</u>, I felt intense pressure to be two different things." (Paragraph 1)

    (1) _____

    (2) _____

    (3)_____

2. "I felt doomed by their pronouncement, misunderstood, and gradually <u>defiant</u>." (3)

    (1) _____

    (2) _____

    (3)_____

3. "My first book was published in 1999, and around then, on the <u>cusp</u> of a new century the term "Indian-American" has become part of this country's vocabulary." (4)

(1) _____

(2) _____

(3)_____

4. "The traditions on either side of the hyphen dwell in me like siblings, still occasionally <u>sparring</u>, one outshining the other depending on the day." (5)

(1) _____

(2) _____

(3)_____

5. "I feel Indian not because of the time I've spent in India or because of my genetic composition but rather because of my parents' <u>steadfast</u> presence in my life." (6)

(1) _____

(2) _____

(3)_____

MY TWO LIVES

—Jhumpa Lahiri

The Pulitzer-winning writer felt intense pressure to be at once 'loyal to the old world and fluent in the new.'

[1]   I have lived in the United States for almost 37 years and anticipate growing old in this country. Therefore, with the exception of my first two years in London, "Indian-American" has been a constant way to describe me. Less constant is my relationship to the term. When I was growing up in Rhode Island in the 1970s, I felt neither Indian nor American. Like many immigrant offspring I felt intense pressure to be two things, loyal to the old world and fluent in the new, approved of on either side of the hyphen. Looking back, I see that this was generally the case. But my perception as a young girl was that I fell short at both ends, shuttling between two dimensions that had nothing to do with one another.

[2]   At home I followed the customs of my parents, speaking Bengali and eating rice and dal with my fingers. These ordinary facts seemed part of a secret, utterly alien way of life, and I took pains to hide them from my American friends. For my parents, home was not our house in Rhode Island but Calcutta, where they were raised. I was aware that the things they lived for—the Nazrul songs they listened to on the reel-to-reel, the family they missed, the clothes my mother wore that were not available in any store in any mall—were at once as precious and as worthless as an outmoded currency.

[3]   I also entered a world my parents had little knowledge or control of: school, books, music, television, things that seeped in and became a fundamental aspect of who I am. I spoke English without an accent, comprehending the language in a way my parents still do not. And yet there was evidence that I was not entirely American. In addition to my distinguishing name and looks, I did not attend Sunday school, did not know how to ice-skate, and disappeared to India for months at a time. Many of these friends proudly called themselves Irish-American or Italian-American. But they were several generations removed from the frequently

humiliating process of immigration, so that the ethnic roots they claimed had descended underground whereas mine were still tangled and green. According to my parents I was not American, nor would I ever be no matter how hard I tried. I felt doomed by their pronouncement, misunderstood, and gradually defiant. In spite of the first lessons of arithmetic, one plus one did not equal two but zero, my conflicting selves always canceling each other out.

[4]   When I first started writing, I was not conscious that my subject was the Indian-American experience. What drew me to my craft was the desire to force the two worlds I occupied to mingle on the page as I was not brave enough, or mature enough, to allow in life. My first book was published in 1999, and around then, on the cusp of a new century, the term "Indian-American" had become part of this country's vocabulary. I've heard it so often that these days, if asked about my background, I use the term myself, pleasantly surprised that I do not have to explain further. What a difference from my early life, when there was no such way to describe me, when the most I could do was to clumsily and ineffectually explain.

[5]   As I approach middle age, one plus one equals two, both in my work and in my daily existence. The traditions on either side of the hyphen dwell in me like siblings, still occasionally sparring, one outshining the other depending on the day. But like siblings, they are intimately familiar with one another, forgiving and intertwined. When my husband and I were married five years ago in Calcutta, we invited friends who had never been to India, and they came full of enthusiasm for a place I avoided talking about in my childhood, fearful of what people might say. Around non-Indian friends, I no longer feel compelled to hide the fact that I speak another language. I speak Bengali to my children, even though I lack the proficiency to teach them to read or write the language. As a child I sought perfection and so denied myself the claim to any identity. As an adult I accept that a bicultural upbringing is a rich but imperfect thing.

[6]   While I am American by virtue of the fact that I was raised in this country, I am Indian thanks to the efforts of two individuals. I feel Indian not because of the time I've spent in India or because of my genetic composition but rather because of my parents' steadfast presence in my life. They live three hours from my home; I speak to them daily and see them about once a month. Everything will change once they die. They will take certain things with them—conversations in another tongue, and perceptions about the difficulties of being foreign. Without them, the back-

and-forth life my family leads, both literally and figuratively, will at last approach stillness. An anchor will drop, and a line of connection will be severed.

[7]   I have always believed that I lack the authority my parents bring to being Indian. But as long as they live, they protect me from feeling like an impostor. Their passing will mark not only the loss of the people who created me but the loss of a singular way of life, a singular struggle. The immigrant's journey, no matter how ultimately rewarding, is founded on departure and deprivation, but it secures for the subsequent generation a sense of arrival and advantage. I can see a day coming when my American side, lacking the counterpoint India has until now maintained, begins to gain ascendancy and weight. It is in fiction that I will continue to interpret the term "Indian-American," calculating that shifting equation, whatever answers it may yield.

THE READING PROCESS

Topics, Main Ideas, and Details

1. What is the topic, or subject of this reading? Use the fewest words possible.

   _____

2. What is the main idea of this text? Underline it if directly stated. Write it in your own words if implied.

   _____

   _____

3. How is the main idea supported in the passage?

   _____

   _____

Identifying Details

Answer the following questions in complete sentences.

1. Who is this article about? Describe the main character.

   _____

   _____

2. How many years has the writer been in the U.S.A.?

   _____

   _____

3. In Paragraph 1, what do you think the word *constant* means?

   _____

   _____

4. How did the writer feel about living in Rhode Island?

   _____

   _____

5. What has changed about her since the time she was a child and the time when she was married?

   _____

   _____

6. Compare and contrast the ways in which the writer feels about herself in childhood vs. adulthood. Be sure to use a contrastive transitional word.

   _____

   _____

Relate to Yourself

Answer the following questions in complete sentences.

1. If you consider yourself an immigrant, how does it feel to you to be hyphenated?

   _____

   _____

2. How does it make you feel when people ask you about your background or accent? Are you embarrassed or proud?

   _____

   _____

Drawing Inferences

The following information is not directly stated in the reading. Infer what the author would say is true. Indicate whether the statement is true or false by writing T or F in the spaces provided.

_____ 1. The author felt very secure being an Indian-American immigrant.

_____ 2. The author feels at home with her hyphenation.

_____ 3. The author's first book was published in the new century.

_____ 4. The author's writing reflected in her inner struggle to live in a western society.

Useful Words/Phrases

1. In Paragraph 1, the author uses *therefore*. What are the words or phrases that can replace the word *therefore*? How does *therefore* function in a sentence?

   _____

   _____

2. In Paragraph 1, the author uses *neither. . . nor*. Write your own sentence by using this phrase.

_____

_____

Idiomatic Expressions

1. In Paragraph 3, the author uses *in spite of*. What are the words or phrases that can replace the phrase *in spite of*? How does *in spite of* function in a sentence?

_____

_____

2. In Paragraph 5, what does *one plus one equals two* mean?

_____

_____

Study Notes: Words That Signal Contrastive Relationship Between Two Ideas

INSPIRATION

but	on the other hand
however	in contrast
on the contrary	although
even though	still
yet	nevertheless
conversely	unlike
while	in spite of
despite	as opposed to
rather than	differently
differs from	instead

Vocabulary Practice

A. Vocabulary Matching

Match the vocabulary words in Column A with their definitions in Column B, and write the correct number in the spaces provided. Refer to the paragraph in the reading for context clues.

Column A		Column B
_____ a. utterly (paragraph 2)		1. a child; children
_____ b. seep	3	2. strong; great
_____ c. anticipate	1	3. box without hitting hard
_____ d. humiliate	3	4. expressed without pause
_____ e. alien	2	5. completely; totally
_____ f. descend	3	6. skill
_____ g. offspring	1	7. expect; foresee; think likely to happen
_____ h. craft	4	8. different; strange
_____ i. precious	2	9. no longer in fashion or use
_____ j. perception	1	10. valuable; of great value
_____ k. cusp	4	11. slowly drifted in; enter
_____ l. spar	5	12. continual; constant
_____ m. shuttle	1	13. to be broken; cut
_____ n. fluent	1	14. understanding; comprehension
_____ o. steadfast	6	15. beginning
_____ p. outmoded	2	16. money
_____ q. sever	6	17. move back and forth
_____ r. impostor	7	18. a person who tries to be someone else by deceiving
_____ s. currency	2	19. go down; fall from a higher level to a lower level
_____ t. intense	1	20. cause to feel ashamed

B. Fill-in-the-Blanks

Choose one of the following words to best complete the sentences below. Some of the words were modified. Use each word only once. Be sure to pay close attention to the context clues provided.

fluent	anticipate	intense

1. You must apply _____ pressure, if you wish to open a jar of pickles.

2. I'm _____ in reading Latin.

3. I _____ the birth of my child.

offspring	constant	shuttle

4. The ebb and flow of the tide are _____.

5. My _____ looks like my husband and myself.

6. Children of divorced parents _____ between two households.

ordinary	utterly	alien

7. During the holidays, we do not eat from _____ tableware.

8. I'm _____ disgusted with the look of my kitchen.

9. The old generations' beliefs are _____ to the new way of thinking.

outmoded	currency	seeped

10. Our _____ consists of nickels, dimes, and quarters.

11. Paging devices have been _____ because of cellular phones and text messaging.

12. The water _____ in through the cracks in the wall.

descended	humiliating	tangled

13. To publically scold your children is _____ for them.

14. The crowds _____ into the horizon.

15. My daughter's hair was _____ after I gave her a bath.

defiant	pronouncement	doomed

16. To be in debt will make you feel _____.

17. The judge gave a final _____ when he/she declared the verdict of not guilty.

18. Children can be _____ when they resist their parents' rules.

craft	mingle	cusp

19. When I go to a party, I try to _____ with other people.

20. Your ability to play with words is your _____.

21. When your birthday is at the end of one month and the beginning of next month, it falls on the _____ of that astrological sign.

POSTREADING

Reading Strategies

Read the questions below and answer in the spaces provided.

1. In reading this passage, what are you reminded of?

   Answer: This reading reminds me of _____

   _____

2. Were you satisfied with your prereading prediction about the text?

   Answer: I was/wasn't satisfied because _____

   _____

3. Do you have any questions about the reading?

   Answer: I wonder _____

   _____

4. What did you visualize while reading this passage?

   Answer: I visualized _____

   _____

5. Is this passage making sense to you?

   Answer: This passage is/isn't making sense to me because _____

   _____

6. What is the main idea of this reading?

   Answer: This reading is about _____

   _____

7. How can you relate the main idea to your own experiences?

   Answer: I can relate this passage to _____

   _____

8. Comment on the author's style of writing.

   Answer: When I read this passage, I feel _____

   _____

9. What have you learned?

   Answer: I have learned _____

   _____

10. During your reading of the text, what appeals to you that you'd like to try in your own writing?

    Answer: In my next writing, I will try _____

    _____

Writing a Summary

Summarize the text in one paragraph, including (1) the title, author of the reading as well as the thesis statement; (2) significant details that support the main idea; and (3) restatement of the main idea in your own words. Note that the purpose of writing a summary is to accurately represent what the author wanted to say, not to provide a critique.

APPLICATION

Internet Activities

1. Locate a writer who is an immigrant descendant to the United States. Find his/her publication that interests you.

   Title: _____

   Author(s): _____

   Publication Date: _____

2. Research why Bengali women dress the way they do.

   _____

   _____

   _____

Reading-response Journal

Write about a time you used a journal to process your conflict. Did it help?

   _____

   _____

   _____

   _____

   _____

   _____

   _____

Study Notes: How to Start Journaling

- Stream of consciousness – Whatever words come to your mind, write them on the paper to help you overcome your fear of starting.

- People use journals to express emotion, take personal inventories, manage feelings, jotting down their personal dreams or goals.

- You can use a journal for a difficult season of life such as grieving a loss.

- It is advisable to keep a personal journal safe from prying eyes.

INSPIRATION

GRAMMAR PRACTICE VIA INTERNET

Go to one of the following websites:

- http://www.sonnerct.com/English_Rules/LR10_Gerunds_Infinitives.htm

- http://grammar.ccc.commnet.edu/grammar/verblist.htm

- http://www.englishpage.com/gerunds/index.htm

- http://www.englisch-hilfen.de/en/exercises/structures/gerund_infinitive_verbs.htm

Research verbs followed by gerunds or infinitives. Write all the verbs that contain gerunds and all that contain infinitives. Identify two sentences in the reading that contain verbs followed by a gerund or an infinitive.

_____

_____

_____

_____

_____

_____

chapter 4

LIFE'S TRAVELS FOR A FATHER AND A SON

PREREADING

Class Discussion

Discuss the following questions in a group.

1. What would be an ideal relationship between a father and a son?

   _____

   _____

   _____

2. What do the pictures on the next page remind you of?

   _____

   _____

   _____

3. Predict what the text will be about by reading the title.

   _____

   _____

   _____

CHAPTER 4: **Life's Travels for a Father and a Son**

4. Predict what the text will be about by reading the first and last paragraphs (See pages 61-64).

_____

_____

_____

5. Write how the author would develop the story.

_____

_____

_____

Vocabulary in Context

Each item below includes a sentence from the reading. Using the context clues from this sentence, (1) determine the part of speech, and (2) formulate your own definition for the underlined word. Then (3) locate the word in a dictionary and write the appropriate definition.

1. "Ben, an avid surfer, had <u>lashed</u> his long board on the roof." (Paragraph 3)

   (1) _____

   (2) _____

   (3)_____

2. "Phil put on two new axles, a tie rod, two used rear tires, and <u>pronounced</u> the Volvo ready." (4)

   (1) _____

   (2) _____

   (3)_____

3. "Starting in mid-August, I asked if, before he left, he would trim the high <u>hedges</u> around our house, a big job." (11)

    (1) _____   ,

    (2) _____

    (3)_____

4. "I found myself wishing the spicy tuna <u>platter</u> would last forever." (16)

    (1) _____

    (2) _____

    (3)_____

5. "He wanted to travel and is happy to work <u>menial</u> jobs for a while." (26)

    (1) _____

    (2) _____

    (3)_____

6. "In the brief moments when I <u>glimpsed</u> him flashing by this summer, I was happy to see he always had a book." (27)

    (1) _____

    (2) _____

    (3)_____

READING

· ·

LIFE'S TRAVELS FOR A FATHER AND A SON

—Michael Winerip

[1]   Ben, my oldest of four children, recently left for his senior year of college. Usually he flies and there's a hurried, confused, curbside goodbye at the airport. This time was different. He was driving the 17 hours to Chicago and our goodbye, in front of the house, felt longer, sadder, more final.

[2]   We'd given him our '98 Volvo station wagon with 168,000 miles. It's a tradition. Some families set up trusts for their children when they graduate; my parents gave me the '68 Chevy Nova with 100,000 miles on it.

[3]   The Volvo was crammed, and Ben, an avid surfer, had lashed his longboard on the roof. It's one of the things I love about him: he's sure he'll find waves in Chicago.

[4]   Before giving him the car, I took it to our mechanic, Phil Kleyn. An engineer in Ukraine before emigrating, he can keep any car on the road. Phil put on two new axles, a tie rod, two used rear tires, and pronounced the Volvo ready.

[5]   "Mikey, call me when he gets to Chicago," Phil said.

[6]   "The car's going to be all right?" I asked.

[7]   "Sure, Mikey, fine, fine," Phil said. "Just call me—you know."

[8]   Ben had been around all summer, but he was never around. Six days a week, he'd work nine-hour shifts as a lifeguard at our Long Island beach. Afterward, he'd stop by the house to eat enormous quantities of food (yet remain criminally skinny), then stay out way past my bedtime. If he had a day off, he'd go into New York City. If he had two days, he'd head to Boston; and five was enough to see Charleston, SC; Wilmington, NC; Washington and Philadelphia. ("We only spent an hour in Philly, Dad, but my friend showed us around and we got a pretty good feel for it.")

[9]   Occasionally he'd sleep 16 hours and wonder why he was tired.

[10]   My wife and I tried getting him to go to a movie with us, but he was way too busy. Or he was certain "Julie & Julia" wasn't going to be his kind of film. Or he'd heard that "500 Days of Summer" was terrific, but the lifeguards were having their third-to-last barbecue of the summer and he really couldn't miss it.

[11]   Starting in mid-August, I asked if, before he left, he would trim the high hedges around our house, a big job. I bought new electric clippers so he could do it right. His college is on the trimester system and he doesn't start until late September. "Right after Labor Day, when I stop lifeguarding," he said.

[12]   After Labor Day, he was going to do it the second week of September, right after his last friends went back to college.

[13]   Two nights before he was to leave, I'm not sure if I was lucky or I made my own luck, but he actually had availability and the two of us went to the Japanese restaurant in town.

[14]   Dinner was fun. He did all the ordering. We each had a couple of beers and I loosened up. We talked about the family, compared notes on the friends he'd brought to visit that summer, joked about the odds of the hedges ever being cut or the Volvo making it out of Pennsylvania.

[15]   It was wonderful and surprising how quickly that feeling of closeness—present daily until they become teenagers—came flooding back.

[16]   I found myself wishing the spicy tuna platter would last forever. I wanted to say something he might remember, but I have had so little success the few times I've tried meaningful talks with my kids. When I tried having the sex talk with Ben when he was in the eighth grade, he was so flustered, I realized it was too early. And when I tried again with Ben in the tenth grade, it was too late. "Don't worry about it, Dad, I'm fine," he told me.

[17]   When he was deciding where to spend his junior year of college abroad, I gave him my talk about having never mastered another language myself and always regretting it, and urged him to pick a Spanish-speaking country. After lis-

tening passively through months of follow-up email messages, he finally sent his response: "Dad, you love Spain so much, you go."

[18]   The photos he posted on Facebook of surfing Australia's east coast were lovely.

[19]   What can a father tell an almost-grown son that might be useful? Does one generation have anything worth telling the next?

[20]   I don't have a clue why, but I told him not to be in a rush to marry. I told him I was glad I'd waited, that a man can wait until he's 35 and still be married 50 years, which seems to be more than enough for everyone involved.

[21]   He appeared to be listening, so I told him while he's young to be with lots of women so when he did marry, he wouldn't feel as if he was missing anything. We both howled. I sounded like the twisted grandfather played by Alan Arkin in "Little Miss Sunshine."

[22]   And I told him the truth, that when I was single I'd never had much luck having casual affairs without creating emotional messes.

[23]   I told him the reason to marry is to have children.

[24]   "Are you glad you had kids?" he asked me. We were walking back to the car by then. I told him it was the best thing I'd ever done.

[25]   He'll be heading out into the worst economy since the Great Depression. When I ask his plans, he's vague. He's been a psychology major and has thought about eventually working in mental health. He mentions Teach for America. He's tired of hunting whitecaps on Lake Michigan and wants to live on a coast again.

[26]   Though his grades are good, he's not applying to law, medical or business schools, as many of his friends are. I admire him for not grabbing at the surest thing. He wants to travel (he says maybe to a Spanish-speaking country this time!) and is happy to work menial jobs for a while. He'll probably be a lifeguard next summer, save his money, then go. I have a lot of confidence in his practical sense and work ethic. He got his first job when he was 12, rising at 5 a.m. to assemble Sunday papers at the corner deli. He applied for a job as a lifeguard on his very first day of college, and has worked each year at the campus pool.

[27]   In the brief moments when I glimpsed him flashing by this summer, I was happy to see he always had a book. He seems to be a lifelong learner, which is what I want most for my children. He seems to understand that the real learning comes after college.

[28]   He was planning on leaving midday Friday, to get out of New York before the afternoon rush hour. He'd been up late doing his laundry and packing the Volvo the night before. He absolutely swore he'd have time to do the hedges that morning before he left.

[29]   Friday morning it was pouring. Cats and dogs. "Can't do the hedges in this," he said. I nodded. "Sorry," he said. I nodded. No point in having him electrocuted. He handed me his eyeglasses. He didn't have time to get them fixed. There were photos he was having printed, that he didn't have time to pick up; medicine that he'd ordered that hadn't arrived.

[30]   "I'll put together in a box and mail it," I said.

[31]   Standing in the driveway in the rain, I told him not to push the Volvo too much, and we hugged. I should be used to it by now, but I'm always caught off guard by the prickliness of the stubble on my three sons' cheeks when we kiss goodbye.

[32]   As I said, the boy has common sense. He broke the trip into three legs, stopping overnight to see friends in Binghamton, NY, and Cleveland. When he reached Chicago, he called. As promised, I called Phil at the garage.

[33]   "Thanks God," Phil said.

[34]   "You told me the car was safe," I said.

[35]   "Of course, of course, Mikey, everything was good, but thanks God."

Study Notes: Narration

- The purpose of a narrative essay is to relate a story about the writer's personal quest.

- The writer should develop a story by chronological order.

- Adverbial clauses of time are useful to enhance coherence.

INSPIRATION

Study Notes: Time Words

when	while
until	often
first	during
second	after
third	eventually
finally	immediately
before	following

INSPIRATION

THE READING PROCESS

Topics, Main Ideas, and Details

1. What is the topic, or subject of this reading? Use the fewest words possible.

   _____

2. What is the main idea of this text? Underline it if directly stated. Write it in your own words if implied.

   _____

   _____

3. How is the main idea supported in the passage?

_____

_____

Identifying Details

Answer the following questions in complete sentences.

1. What did the father notice whenever he caught a glimpse of his son?

   _____

   _____

2. What was Ben's major in college?

   _____

   _____

3. What favor was asked of Ben by his father?

   _____

   _____

4. Where did Ben and his family go for dinner?

   _____

   _____

5. What three stops did Ben make on his way to Chicago?

   _____

   _____

6. What did the mechanic do to the Volvo that Ben was to drive to Chicago?

_____

_____

7. How often and how long did Ben work?

_____

_____

8. Where did Ben go to study abroad?

_____

_____

9. Give one example of the relationship Ben had with his father as a teen.

_____

_____

Open-ended Questions

Answer the following questions in complete sentences.

1. What was your parents' reaction upon beginning your freshman college year?

_____

_____

2. Can you come up with a different title for this article?

_____

_____

Drawing Inferences

What can you infer about the relationship Ben has with his father? Give two brief statements that support your answer.

_____

_____

_____

Useful Words/Phrases

1. In Paragraph 14, the author uses a phrase, *loosen up*. What are the words or phrases that can replace the verb phrase? What do they mean?

   _____

   _____

2. In Paragraph 22, the author uses a phrase, *emotional messes*. How would you describe it?

   _____

   _____

Idiomatic Expressions

In Paragraph 29, what does it mean by *cats and dogs*?

_____

Vocabulary Practice

A. Multiple Choice

Using the context clues from each sentence below, choose the best definition for the under-lined word, and circle the appropriate answer letter.

1. The ice cream man sold his goods at the <u>curbside</u>.

    a. in the middle of the road

    b. in the street

    c. at the edge of the street, near the corner

2. The college students <u>crammed</u> all night for their finals.

    a. stuffed their minds

    b. stuffed their cars

    c. stuffed their suitcases

3. My night table has piles of books because I am an <u>avid</u> reader.

    a. My room is messy.

    b. I read a lot.

    c. I sleep in a library.

4. The snake <u>lashed</u> its body around its prey.

    a. tied securely

    b. ate it whole

    c. drained its blood

5. The judge <u>pronounced</u> the couple man and wife.

    a. decided

    b. discussed

    c. declared

6. They do not lock up prisoners who are <u>criminally</u> insane with normal prisoners.

   a. extremely

   b. rarely

   c. ridiculously

7. We have many green <u>hedges</u> around our house.

   a. shrubs which act as a fence

   b. a white picket fence

   c. a moat with alligators

8. When the professor caught me cheating I became very <u>flustered</u>.

   a. excited

   b. disgusted

   c. embarrassed

9. Although scrubbing toilets is a <u>menial</u> task, it is a job someone has to do.

   a. high-paying job

   b. requiring little skill

   c. professional work

10. Through the corner of my eye, I caught a <u>glimpse</u> of my daughter boarding the plane.

    a. a long staring gaze

    b. making eye-contact

    c. a brief glance for a moment

B. Fill-in-the-Blanks

Choose one of the following words to best complete the sentences below. Some of the words were modified. Use each word only once. Be sure to pay close attention to the context clues provided.

avid	cram	lashed

1. When my son was told to clean up his room, he began to _____ everything into his toy box.

2. Bob, being an ___a___ reader of the *New York Times*, was always up to date with current events.

3. The campers made sure that the camping supplies were properly _l_____ to their backs before starting their hike.

emigrated	longboard	axles

4. The surfers were seen carrying their ___l_____ along the beach.

5. After mass lay-offs, many of the former employees _e_____ to somewhere cheaper.

6. The wheels detached from the _a_____ and rolled away.

hedges	pronounced	criminally

7. The priest ___p_____ the lovely couple husband and wife.

8. The young girl was ___c_____ clumsy and always hurt herself.

9. The ___h_____ were perfectly manicured and very well kept.

platter	flustered	howled

10. He took his _____ to the lunch table and ate with his friends.

11. Our friends told us a funny joke and we _____.

12. The young girl became _____ when her crush asked her out.

glimpse	assembled	menial

13. Such a __menial__ task can be so tedious.

14. The new employee quickly _____ his paperwork and presented it to his manager.

15. I managed to _____ the little boy's hiding spot but I didn't say a thing.

prickliness	legs

16. After a day without shaving, the _____ of his chin was more than his girl-friend could stand.

17. The trip was divided into five _____ so we could stop and rest.

POSTREADING

Reading Strategies

Read the questions below and answer in the spaces provided.

1. In reading this passage, what are you reminded of?

   Answer: This reading reminds me of _____

   _____

2. Were you satisfied with your prereading prediction about the text?

   Answer: I was/wasn't satisfied because _____

   _____

3. Do you have any questions about the reading?

   Answer: I wonder _____

   _____

4. What did you visualize while reading this passage?

   Answer: I visualized _____

   _____

5. Is this passage making sense to you?

   Answer: This passage is/isn't making sense to me because _____

   _____

6. What is the main idea of this reading?

   Answer: This reading is about _____

   _____

7. How can you relate the main idea to your own experiences?

   Answer: I can relate this passage to _____

   _____

8. Comment on the author's style of writing.

   Answer: When I read this passage, I feel _____

   _____

9. What have you learned?

   Answer: I have learned _____

   _____

10. During your reading of the text, what appeals to you that you'd like to try in your own writing?

    Answer: In my next writing I will try _____

    _____

Writing a Summary

Summarize the text in one paragraph, including (1) the title, author of the reading as well as the thesis statement; (2) significant details that support the main idea; and (3) restate the main idea in your own words. Note that the purpose of writing a summary is to accurately represent what the author wanted to say, not to provide a critique.

_____

_____

_____

_____

_____

_____

_____

_____

_____

APPLICATION . . . .

Internet Activities

1. Find out more about teachforamerica.com. What does it do?

_____

_____

_____

2. Search for some popular surfing places in the U.S./internationally and share your findings with your classmates.

_____

_____

_____

Reading-response Journal

What advice could a parent tell his/her almost grown-up young adult that might be useful? Does one generation have anything worth telling the next? Write your responses.

_____

_____

_____

_____

_____

_____

_____

_____

_____

_____

_____

_____

GRAMMAR PRACTICE VIA INTERNET

Go to one of the following websites:

- http://www.englishpage.com/verbpage/verbtenseintro.html

- http://leo.stcloudstate.edu/grammar/tenses.html

- http://owl.english.purdue.edu/owl/resource/601/01/

Research these tenses on the Internet: *simple past*, *past progressive*, and *past perfect*. Write the definition for each on the lines provided.

Identify a sentence for each tense in the reading. Write the verb and discuss its function on the lines below.

_____

_____

_____

_____

_____

_____

_____

_____

_____

_____

_____

unit 3
PEOPLE AND SOCIETY

chapter 5

FINDING A HOME AT LAST

PREREADING

· ·

Class Discussion

Discuss the following questions in a group.

1. Do you like your own home? What do you like about it?

_____

_____

_____

2. What do the pictures on the next page remind you of?

_____

_____

_____

3. Predict what the text will be about by reading the title.

_____

_____

_____

34,675: New York's homeless population as estimated by the city.

Image © Arman Zhenikeyev, 2012. Shutterstock, Inc.

4. Predict what the text will be about by reading the first and last paragraphs (See pages 84-86).

_____

_____

_____

_____

_____

5. Write how the author would develop the story.

Image © Paula k, 2012. Shutterstock, Inc.

_____

_____

_____

Vocabulary in Context

Each item below includes a sentence from the reading. Using the context clues from this sentence, (1) determine the part of speech, and (2) formulate your own definition for the underlined word. Then (3) locate the word in a dictionary and write the appropriate definition.

1. "New York <u>pioneers</u> new way of getting people off the street." (Subtitle)

    (1) _____

    (2)_____

    (3)_____

2. "A recovering heroin <u>addict</u> in a methadone program, Miyares has been homeless for a few years." (Paragraph 2)

    (1) _____

    (2)_____

    (3)_____

3. "That concept, known as the 'Housing First' principle, once considered <u>unorthodox</u>, is gaining acceptance across that nation." (4)

    (1) _____

    (2)_____

    (3)_____

4. "As she shops for groceries, towels, and other <u>necessities</u>, Miyares is thinking more about her footwear than the fact that she is going to be living in her own place for the first time in her 44 years." (9)

    (1) _____

    (2)_____

    (3)_____

5. "That <u>radical</u> yet obvious idea that the best way to tackle homelessness is to give people homes." (14)

(1) _____

(2)_____

(3)_____

6. "A bed in a state <u>psychiatric</u> hospital costs an estimated $175,000 a year." (In the Box)

(1) _____

(2)_____

(3)_____

READING
· ·

FINDING A HOME AT LAST

—Michael Clancy

New York pioneers new way of getting people off the street

[1]   Maria Miyares' feet are killing her. She needs a new pair of shoes. She also needs a glass table. She needs a microwave. She needs to kick her drug habit.

[2]   A recovering heroin addict in a methadone program, Miyares has been homeless for a few years, living in prison, shelters, and with friends.

[3]   For the first time in her life, she has her own apartment because of Pathways to Housing, an organization that operates under the principle that people need homes before they can successfully overcome mental illness or addiction.

[4]   That concept, known as the "Housing First" principle, once considered unorthodox, is gaining acceptance across the nation. The Bush administration has

embraced the idea because not only do studies show it helps people stay off the street, but because it is often cheaper for taxpayers.

[5]   The Housing First concept, born in New York, has spread across the nation from Philadelphia to Denver to Seattle. As the city Department of Homeless Services tries to make good on Mayor Michael Bloomberg's pledge to reduce street homelessness by two-thirds before his term is over, it could be expanded here.

[6]   "We will not get there with business as usual," said department Commissioner Robert Hess.

[7]   Pathways helps more than 400 formerly homeless people in the city maintain a permanent home with an 88% retention rate.

[8]   "The research holds true in New York," Hess said. "And I can tell you from experience in Philadelphia, if you move someone from under a bridge, even if they've been living there for 15 years, to an apartment ... they will be a good neighbor."

[9]   As she shops for groceries, towels, and other necessities, Miyares is thinking more about her footwear than the fact that she is going to be living in her own place for the first time in her 44 years. As a van takes her to her new place in the Allerton section of the Bronx, the reality of it all hasn't set in.

[10]   "My brother-in-law is a chef; my sister is a nurse; my niece is a cop," she said before pausing to add, "And I'm a bum."

[11]   "You're not a bum," said a Pathways to Housing counselor.

[12]   "But I'm homeless," she said.

[13]   "Not anymore," came the reply.

[14]   That radical yet obvious idea that the best way to tackle homelessness is to give people homes started as a research project in New York City in 1993. Pathways to Housing pioneered the approach that said housing need not be tied to counseling.

[15]   "We try and take people as they are," said Ed Rooney, a case manager who has been with the group since its inception. "We will work on their issues once they are housed—not the other way around."

[16]   For Miyares, she's got to complete her methadone therapy and then find a job. It's a long road but one that's been walked by others before her. But just having

her own place has lifted her spirit, despite whatever issues she has to overcome.

[17]   "There's nothing like home, sweet home," she said, "and I've got mad closets."

Making Common (and Fiscal) Sense

Housing First's approach to fighting homelessness is gaining popularity not only because it is effective, but because it can save taxpayers money.

For example, the top 25 recipients of Medicaid dollars for detoxification cost taxpayers $4.1 million in the fiscal year 2003-04, according to the state Office of Alcoholism and Substance Abuse Services (OASAS). During that same period, the No. 1 recipient of Medicaid-funded detox dollars spent 204 days in detox through 21 different stays at hospitals from Coney Island to midtown. That one person's detox alone cost taxpayers &240,743 in one fiscal year.

A Pathways apartment along with support and counseling services costs an average of $22,500 per client each year. A bed in a state psychiatric hospital costs an estimated $175,000 a year.

THE READING PROCESS

Topics, Main Ideas, and Details

1. What is the topic, or subject of this reading? Use the fewest words possible.

    _____

2. What is the main idea of this text? Underline it if directly stated. Write it in your own words if implied.

    _____

    _____

3. How is the main idea supported in the passage?

    _____

    _____

Identifying Details

Answer the following questions in complete sentences.

1. Describe Maria Miyares. What kind of person is she?

   _____

   _____

   _____

2. Define Pathways to Housing. What are the functions of the organization? How is the organization tied to counseling?

   _____

   _____

   _____

3. Who is the "Housing First" concept for?

   _____

   _____

   _____

4. During which administration was the plan adopted?

   _____

   _____

   _____

5. Why has the administration supported the "Housing First" principle?

   _____

   _____

   _____

6. What was the retention rate of the housing program?

_____

_____

_____

7. How much money did the top 25 recipients of Medicaid money cost taxpayers in the years 2003-2004?

_____

_____

_____

Open-ended Questions

1. What was the author's purpose in writing this article?

_____

_____

_____

2. How does Maria Miyares feel about having her own home?

_____

_____

_____

Drawing Inferences

The following information is not directly stated in the reading. Indicate whether the statement is true or false by writing T or F in the spaces provided.

___ 1. Maria Miyares has a well-furnished apartment from the Housing First Program.

___ 2. The Housing first concept is predominantly located in New York.

___ 3. Maria Miyares was homeless because of default mortgage.

___ 4. Medicaid funds for heroin addicts.

Useful Words/Phrases

1. In Paragraph 4, the author uses a phrase *not only . . . but (also)*. Write your own sentence by using this expression.

   _____

   _____

2. Find how the author uses the word *despite* in Paragraph 16. Write its part of speech and meaning. Write your own sentence by using the word.

   _____

   _____

Idiomatic Expressions

1. In Paragraph 1, what does it mean by *kick her drug habit*?

   _____

   _____

   _____

2. In Paragraph 9, the author uses a verb phrase *set in*. What does it mean? Write your own sentence by using this phrase.

_____

_____

Vocabulary Practice

Match the underlined words with their definitions in the box. Write the appropriate answer letter in the spaces provided.

____D____ 1. Many of the drug <u>addicts</u> in the rehabilitation center were being treated for multiple issues.

_____ 2. Her <u>unorthodox</u> methods often draw dirty looks, but she ignores them.

_____ 3. If you put your mind to it, you can <u>overcome</u> any obstacle that stands in your way!

_____ 4. With the start of the new year, Bob <u>pledged</u> to stop eating so much junk food.

_____ 5. Once I presented the marketing strategy to the CEO, she <u>embraced</u> the idea.

_____ 6. There are many types of <u>addictions</u> and some are more subtle than others.

_____ 7. The city council planned to <u>expand</u> the school to accommodate the influx of new students.

_____ 8. The former pop singer was brought to the hospital for <u>detoxification</u>.

_____ 9. Tired of being called a <u>bum</u>, Bill got cleaned up and got a steady job.

_____ 10. Once the plan was set up, we went about <u>tackling</u> the issue at hand.

_____ 11. The <u>retention rate</u> of new employees rose after the company improved the work environment.

_____ 12. Many of the children on the <u>psychiatric</u> hospital had emotional disorders such as depression.

_____ 13. As soon as I heard the good news, my spirits were <u>lifted</u> instantly.

_____ 14. Many of the senior members were in the organization since its <u>inception</u>.

_____ 15. The primary <u>recipients</u> of the grant money will be children from under-
privileged families.

a. different from what is usually done or expected

b. to take up especially readily or gladly

c. to make larger

d. one who is dependent on a substance or activity

e. the amount of keeping someone or something usually measured in percentages

f. to promise

g. to get the better of

h. persistent compulsive use of a substance known by the user to be harmful

i. pertaining to mental, emotional, or behavioral disorders

j. one who sponges off others and avoids work

k. to set about dealing with

l. to raise or make higher

m. one who receives

n. an act, or instance of beginning

o. the process of removing a harmful substance from one's body (i.e., drugs)

POSTREADING

Reading Strategies

Read the questions below and answer in the spaces provided.

1. In reading this passage, what are you reminded of?

   Answer: This reading reminds me of _____

   _____

2. Were you satisfied with your prereading prediction about the text?

   Answer: I was/wasn't satisfied because _____

   _____

3. Do you have any questions about the reading?

   Answer: I wonder _____

   _____

4. What did you visualize while reading this passage?

   Answer: I visualized _____

   _____

5. Is this passage making sense to you?

   Answer: This passage is/isn't making sense to me because _____

   _____

6. What is the main idea of this reading?

   Answer: This reading is about _____

   _____

7. How can you relate the main idea to your own experiences?

   Answer: I can relate this passage to _____

   _____

8. Comment on the author's style of writing.

   Answer: When I read this passage, I feel _____

   _____

9. What have you learned?

   Answer: I have read _____

   _____

10. During your reading of the text, what appeals to you that you'd like to try in your own writing?

    Answer: In my next writing I will try _____

    _____

Practice Makes Perfect!

Read the paragraph below and answer the questions that follow.

> (1) I support drug rehabilitation programs to take homeless drug addicts off the street. (2) My first reason is that many modern drug rehabilitation programs are extremely effective in reversing addiction. (3) Several research studies have shown that with proper medication, counseling, and group therapy; drug addiction can be eliminated. (4) My second reason for supporting drug rehabilitation is that it is far less expensive in the long run than rent-free housing. (5) Many drug rehabilitation programs can accomplish their goal within 3-6 months, whereas rent-free housing can go on many years. (6) My third reason is that drug rehabilitation programs provide a social network for recovering addicts. (7) Since addicts are isolated and considered social outcasts, it is important for them to meet both individuals who have kicked the habit as well as people like themselves struggling to overcome their addiction. (8) For these three reasons and explanations offered, I support drug rehabilitation for homeless drug addicts.

1. Formulate your title for this reading.

   _____

2. What is the topic, or subject of this reading? Use the fewest words possible.

   _____

3. What is the main idea of this text? Underline it if directly stated. Write it in your own words if implied.

   _____

   _____

4. How is the main idea supported in the passage?

_____

_____

Now that you've completed reading comprehension questions, we are moving toward writing. The passage you just read is indeed a model paragraph written based on the essay topic below.

Write *your* paragraph now! The model paragraph should give you some ideas as to how to write your own.

Topic: New York City has recently received funding to take homeless drug addicts off the street. Two proposals have been suggested. One is to provide them rent-free housing and the other is to provide money to place them in a drug rehabilitation program.

Write a paragraph that supports the following proposal: "New York City should use recent funding to provide rent-free housing to take homeless drug addicts off the street."

Your paragraph should only contain the following eight sentence outline. Please number each sentence before you write it.

1st sentence – State your position.

2nd sentence – State reason #1 for taking your position.

3rd sentence – Explain, using examples, reason #1.

4th sentence – State reason #2 for taking your position.

5th sentence – Explain, using examples, reason #2.

6th sentence – State reason #3 for taking your position.

7th sentence – Explain, using examples, reason #3.

8th sentence – Conclusion.

_____

_____

_____

_____

_____

_____

_____

_____

_____

APPLICATION
· ·

Internet Activities

1. Learn more about Pathways to Housing by clicking on

    http://www.pathwaystohousing.org/

    Find out how the recipients of "Housing First" are selected.

    _____

    _____

    _____

2. Check out the city Department of Homeless Services website. List four services they provide homeless patrons.

_____

_____

_____

Reading-response Journal

What does your home represent to you? Give sufficient details in your response.

_____

_____

_____

_____

_____

_____

_____

_____

_____

_____

_____

_____

_____

Building Critical Thinking

Read carefully the following model letter supporting drug rehabilitation for the homeless.

Sample Letter

Dear Mayor Bloomberg:

I'm writing to you to offer my reasons for providing drug rehabilitation for the homeless drug addicts of New York City. I believe drug rehabilitation is the most effective approach to help both drug addicts and the city of New York.

My first reason for providing drug rehabilitation is that this approach directly attacks the individual's drug addiction and has the best chance of success in helping the addict overcome his dependency. Research has indicated that while counseling may be beneficial, there is no substitute for a drug rehabilitation program.

Second, I would argue that a drug rehabilitation program for 24 hours a day, 7 days a week would reduce virtually all crime committed by drug addicts because now they are confined in a rehabilitation setting. Addicts would not be released until they had overcome their addiction and are ready to return to society as productive citizens. Our city's residents and tourists would very much welcome this change.

In conclusion, even though drug rehabilitation may prove more costly than other alternatives in the short run, this investment of limited city funds will prove most effective in the long term.

Sincerely,

[your name]

Have you ever written a letter to a politician? Write a letter to Mayor Bloomberg explaining your reasons to support the other position: Rent-free Housing for homeless drug addicts. Explain why this approach is more effective to help both these people and the city of New York. The model letter should give you some ideas as to how to write your own letter supporting this position. Start writing a letter!

_____

_____

_____

_____

_____

_____

_____

_____

_____

_____

_____

_____

Study Notes: Writing an Opinion Letter

- Opinions are based on issues, not people or businesses.

- Use encouraging words to support your opinion.

- Support your findings with facts and solid evidence.

- Review facts and information prior to submitting your opinion.

INSPIRATION

GRAMMAR PRACTICE VIA INTERNET

Go to one of the following websites:

- http://leo.stcloudstate.edu/grammar/subverag.html

- http://www.grammarbook.com/grammar/subjectVerbAgree.asp

Research what *subject-verb agreement* is and write the definition. Choose a sentence from the reading and write how the subject agrees with the verb on the lines below.

_____

_____

_____

_____

_____

_____

_____

_____

_____

_____

_____

_____

_____

_____

chapter 6

IMMIGRATION STORIES, FROM SHADOWS TO SPOTLIGHT

PREREADING

Class Discussion

Discuss the following questions in a group.

1. Do you know anything about your family's history? Where did your ancestors come from?

   _____

   _____

   _____

2. What do the pictures on the next page remind you of?

   _____

   _____

   _____

3. Predict what the text will be about by reading the title.

   _____

   _____

   _____

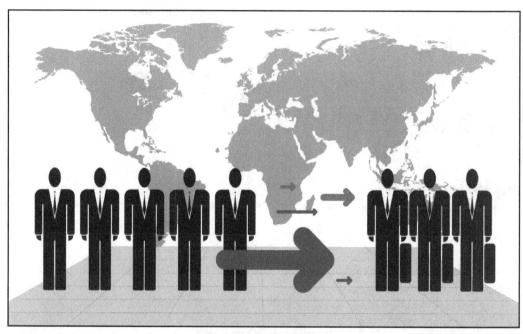

CHAPTER 6: **Immigration Stories, from Shadows to Spotlight**

4. Predict what the text will be about by reading the first and last paragraphs (See pages 104-107).

_____

_____

5. Write how the author would develop the story.

_____

_____

Vocabulary in Context

Each item below includes a sentence from the reading. Using the context clues from this sentence, (1) determine the part of speech, and (2) formulate your own definition for the underlined word. Then (3) locate the word in a dictionary and write the appropriate definition.

1. Mr. Hom, a New York laundry worker who helped build battleships in World War II and put three children through college, outlived the <u>stigma</u> of an earlier era's immigration fraud. (Paragraph 2)

   (1) _____

   (2) _____

   (3)_____

2. The book traces how today's national <u>apparatus</u> of immigration restriction was created and shaped by efforts to keep out Chinese workers. (4)

   (1) _____

   (2) _____

   (3)_____

3. When his memory was still sharp, his daughter Dorothy <u>transcribed</u> 48 pages of his taped recollections, which became the basis of a four-minute first-person narrative produced by the museum. (8)

(1) _____

(2) _____

(3)_____

4. Unlike any other immigrant group, the Chinese were <u>barred</u> from naturalizing. (13)

(1) _____

(2) _____

(3)_____

5. That finding <u>reverberates</u> today, said Daniel Kanstroom, a legal scholar and the author of "Deportation Nation." (16)

(1) _____

(2) _____

(3)_____

READING

. . . .

IMMIGRATION STORIES, FROM SHADOWS TO SPOTLIGHT

—Nina Bernstein

[1]   Frail and dignified at 88, the man leaned on his cane and smiled as the story of his immigration in 1936 flashed behind him on a museum wall. Like tens of

From <u>New York Times</u>, September 30, 2009, NY Edition by Nina Bernstein. Copyright © 2009 by New York Times. Reprinted by permission.

thousands of others who managed to come to the United States from China during a 60-year period when the law singled them out for exclusion, the man, Tun Funn Hom, had entered as a "paper son," with false identity papers that claimed his father was a native citizen.

[2]   For years, it was a shameful family secret. But Mr. Hom, a New York laundry worker who helped build battleships in World War II and put three children through college, outlived the stigma of an earlier era's immigration fraud.

[3]   A narrow legalization program let him reclaim his true name in the 1950s. His life story is now on permanent display at the Museum of Chinese in America, which reopened last week at 215 Centre Street. And it illuminates an almost forgotten chapter in American history, one that historians say has new relevance in the current crackdown on illegal immigration.

[4]   "When we think about illegal immigration, we think about Mexican immigrants, whereas in fact illegal immigration cuts across all immigrant groups," said Erika Lee, the author of *At America's Gate: Chinese Immigration During the Exclusion Era, 1882-1943*. The book traces how today's national apparatus of immigration restriction was created and shaped by efforts to keep out Chinese workers and to counter the tactics they developed to overcome the barriers.

[5]   "The current parallels are striking," said Professor Lee, who teaches history at the University of Minnesota. And though some descendants of paper sons do not make the connection, many others have become immigrant rights advocates in law, politics, or museums like this one, which hopes to draw a national audience to its new Chinatown space, designed by Maya Lin.

[6]   "In the Chinese-American community, it has only been very recently that these types of histories have been made public," Professor Lee said. "Even my own grandparents who came in as paper sons were very, very reluctant to talk about this."

[7]   For Mr. Hom, who was a teenager when he arrived to work in his father's laundry on Bleecker Street, the past is now a blur. "It was so long ago that I hardly remember," he said, as his wife, Yoke Won Hom, 82, straightened the lapels of his suit for a photograph.

[8]   But when his memory was still sharp, his daughter Dorothy transcribed 48 pages of his taped recollections, which became the basis of a four-minute first-person narrative produced by the museum. It is one of 10 such autobiographical videos that form the museum's core exhibit.

[9]   "To get into the U.S. under the laws back then, I had to pretend to be another person," Mr. Hom wrote. His father had bought him immigration papers that included 32 pages of information he was to memorize in preparation for hours of interrogation at Ellis Island.

[10]   Such cheat sheets were part of an elaborate, self-perpetuating cycle of enforcement and evasion, historians say. The authorities kept ratcheting up their scrutiny and requirements for documents, feeding a lucrative network of fraud and official corruption as immigrants tried to show they were either merchants or native-born citizens, groups exempt from the exclusion laws.

[11]   Mr. Hom was allowed ashore as Hom Ngin Sing, a student and son of a native. In reality, his father had made it to the United States only about six years earlier, through a similar subterfuge, like an estimated 90 percent of Chinese immigrants of the period.

[12]   Like many poor families from Taishan, a region that sent many emigrants to California during the Gold Rush of 1849, the Homs had deep ties to the United States. Mr. Hom's great-uncle, for example, died in the San Francisco earthquake of 1906.

[13]   But unlike any other immigrant group, the Chinese were barred from naturalizing. That bar was part of the Chinese Exclusion Act, which was passed in 1882 after years of escalating anti-Chinese violence in the West spurred by recessions, labor strife, and a culture of white supremacy.

[14]   The law was expanded in 1892 with a measure that required all Chinese to register with the government and subjected them to deportation unless they proved legal residency, which required the testimony of at least one white witness.

[15]   In a comment that reflected the tone in Congress, one senator asserted that the government had the right "to set apart for them, as we have for the Indians, a territory or reservation, where they should not break out to contaminate our people."

[16] Lawyers argued that the law was repugnant to "the very soul of the Constitution." But it was upheld in a sweeping Supreme Court decision of 1893, Fong Yue Ting v. United States, which held that the government's power to deport foreigners, whether here legally or not, was as "absolute and unqualified" as the power to exclude them. That finding reverberates today, said Daniel Kanstroom, a legal scholar and the author of *Deportation Nation*.

[17] Long after exclusion laws were repealed by Congress in 1943, after China became a World War II ally, that vast power over noncitizens was deployed in raids against immigrants of various ethnic groups whose politics were considered subject.

[18] In the 1950s, Mr. Hom and his relatives, like many Chinese New Yorkers, suddenly faced the exposure of their false papers in just such an operation. The government was tipped off by an informer in Hong Kong as part of a cold war effort to stop illegal immigration.

[19] "We were very scared," said Mrs. Hom, who worked at the family's laundry, first in the Bronx, then in Bay Ridge, Brooklyn. "Everybody was very worried on account maybe they all be sent back to China."

[20] But in a government "confession program," Mr. Hom and some of his relatives admitted their illegal entry; because Mr. Hom had served in the military, he received citizenship papers within months.

[21] As someone who never made it to high school, he now beams over his children's professional successes and his six multiethnic grandchildren. His son, Tom, is a dentist in Manhattan; his daughter Mary is a physician in the Syracuse area, and Dorothy, an interior designer, works with her husband, Michael Strauss, a principal with Vanguard Construction, which recently completed DBGB Kitchen and Bar, Daniel Boulud's latest restaurant.

[22] At a time when debates about immigration often include the claim that "my relatives came the legal way," referring to a period when there were few restrictions on any immigrants except the Chinese, the Hom family has a different perspective.

[23] "One's status being legal or illegal, it's two seconds apart at any point," Dorothy said. "For some, the process is more difficult than others."

THE READING PROCESS

Topics, Main Ideas, and Details

1. What is the topic, or subject of this reading? Use the fewest words possible.

   _____

2. What is the main idea of this text? Underline it if directly stated. Write it in your own words if implied.

   _____

   _____

3. How is the main idea supported in the passage?

   _____

   _____

Identifying Details

Answer the following questions in complete sentences.

1. Who is this article about? Describe the main character.

   _____

   _____

2. Why did the Chinese have to use fake documents to get into the United States?

   _____

   _____

3. Why was the law repealed by Congress in 1943?

_____

_____

4. How many pages of information did Mr. Hom have to memorize for the interrogation on Ellis Island?

_____

_____

5. Why did the Chinese Exclusion Act take place?

_____

_____

6. When did Mr. Hom finally have the chance to reclaim his real name?

_____

_____

7. How long did it take for Mr. Hom to get his citizenship papers and why?

_____

_____

8. When was the Chinese Exclusion Act repealed?

_____

_____

9. Why was the Chinese Exclusion Act researched and reviewed after 50 years?

_____

_____

Relate to Yourself

Answer the following questions in complete sentences.

1. If you consider yourself an immigrant, is there a shameful stigma attached to your identity?

   _____

   _____

2. What television role models portray successful immigrants in America?

   _____

   _____

Drawing Inferences

The following information is not directly stated in the reading. Infer what the author would say is true. Indicate whether the statement is true or false by writing T or F in the spaces provided.

_____ 1. Ellis Island was an immigration station in which many newly arrived immigrants passed through.

_____ 2. A paper son is a person with their identity on paper only.

_____ 3. Mr. Hom's attitude toward his Chinese heritage surpassed his children's professional capability.

_____ 4. In retrospect, the government's confession program allowed Mr. Hom to receive his citizenship papers.

_____ 5. Mr. Hom's memoirs were impaired due to dementia.

Useful Words/Phrases

1. In Paragraph 7, the author uses *hardly*. What are the words or phrases that can replace the word *hardly*? How do they function in sentences?

   _____

   _____

2. In Paragraph 13, the author uses *unlike*. Write your own sentence by using this preposition.

   _____

   _____

Idiomatic Expressions

1. In Paragraph 7, what does it mean by . . . *is a blur*?

   _____

2. In Paragraph 16, what is meant by *the very sole of*? What are the words or phrases that can replace this phrase?

   _____

3. In Paragraph 18, what does it mean by *tip off*? What are the words or phrases that can replace this phrase? Write your own sentence using this phrase.

   _____

Vocabulary Practice

Fill-in-the-Blanks

Choose one of the following words to best complete the sentences below. Some of the words were modified. Use each word only once. Be sure to pay close attention to the context clues provided.

dignified	frail	flash

1. Memories continued to ___Flash___ in the man's head as he lay in his bed.

2. The ___frail___ noble kept quiet even while being barraged with insults from his sister.

3. The pot was so ___dignified___ that a soft poke could cause a crack.

relevance	illuminate	exclusion

4. During the 60-year period of ___exclusion___, the family managed to sneak into the country.

5. That is hardly a matter of ___relevance___ to the current situation.

6. After some research, he was able to ___illuminate___ the subject of his study.

descendant	tactics	counter

7. In an argument, it is important that you ___counter___ with a level headed rebuttal.

8. The ___descendant___ of the military general was promised a very generous pension.

9. The S.W.A.T team's ___tactics___ are designed for quick action.

advocate	parallel	overcome

10. With a bit of hope we can __overcome__ any adversity.

11. The two wars seem to run __parallel__ in tendency and strategies.

12. The Congressman was a known __advocate__ for gay marriage.

perpetuate	reluctant	blur

13. She did all she could to __perpetuate__ her name.

14. He was __reluctant__ to tell the truth knowing what the consequences may be.

15. Her whole weekend was a __blur__.

ratchet	lapel	interrogation

16. He had a rose pinned to his __lapel__ during the prom.

17. The police conducted an __interrogation__ on the suspect but to no avail.

18. They continued to __ratchet__ their search attempts till they found the missing person.

escalating	evasion	scrutiny

19. The __evasion__ of the question was ineffective and eventually she answered it.

20. The __escalating__ debate soon became an all-out fist fight.

21. The detective's __scrutiny__ discovered many clues.

spurred	barred	subterfuge

22. Many immigrants use _subterfuge_ in order to enter different countries.

23. We were _spurred_ from achieving our dreams.

24. The rash actions were _barred_ by the people's fed-up attitude.

asserted	strife	supremacy

25. Our _strife_ was so horrid that it even made the news.

26. She _asserted_ that she had no intention on leaving home.

27. His ideals of _supremacy_ were ultimately his downfall.

contaminate	testimony	deportation

28. The witness gave _testimony_ to the victim's story.

29. The immigrants eventually had to go through the process of _deportation_.

30. We were worried that he might _contaminate_ the others so we separated him from them.

sweeping	upheld	repugnant

31. A _sweeping_ decision instantly passed the law with little hesitation.

32. The odor coming from the garbage can was _repugnant_.

33. The law must be _upheld_ no matter what.

raid	ally	reverberated

34. His yells _reverberated_ throughout the house.

35. The _raid_ to clear out the rebels was successful.

36. Never cheat or deceive an _ally_.

deployed	vast	beamed

37. Her father _beamed_ at her from the audience.

38. The _vast_ power of citizens' voices is very underestimated.

39. All units were _deployed_ in response to the bomb threat.

POSTREADING

Reading Strategies

Read the questions below and answer in the spaces provided.

1. In reading this passage, what are you reminded of?

   Answer: This reading reminds me of _____

   _____

2. Were you satisfied with your prereading prediction about the text?

   Answer: I was/wasn't satisfied because _____

   _____

3. Do you have any questions about the reading?

   Answer: I wonder _____

   _____

4. What did you visualize while reading this passage?

   Answer: I visualized _____

   _____

5. Is this passage making sense to you?

   Answer: This passage is/isn't making sense to me because _____

   _____

6. What is the main idea of this reading?

   Answer: This reading is about _____

   _____

7. How can you relate the main idea to your own experiences?

   Answer: I can relate this passage to _____

   _____

8. Comment on the author's style of writing.

   Answer: When I read this passage, I feel _____

   _____

9. What have you learned?

   Answer: I have learned _____

   _____

10. During your reading of the text, what appeals to you that you'd like to try in your own writing?

Answer: In my next writing I will try _____

_____

Writing a Summary

Summarize the text in one paragraph, including (1) the title, author of the reading as well as the thesis statement; (2) significant details that support the main idea; and (3) restatement of the main idea in your own words. Note that the purpose of writing a summary is to accurately represent what the author wanted to say, not to provide a critique.

_____

_____

_____

_____

_____

_____

_____

_____

_____

_____

_____

_____

_____

APPLICATION

Internet Activities

1. Find out how to legally immigrate to America and share your findings with your classmates.

   _____

   _____

   _____

2. Explore Ellis Island's immigration history and share your findings with your classmates.

   _____

   _____

   _____

3. Find out what the Chinese Exclusion Act is about. Share your findings with your classmates.

   _____

   _____

   _____

Reading-response Journal

In what way does your family provide for you morally during your academic career? Do your parents' academic expectations match those of your own?

_____

_____

_____

_____

_____

_____

_____

_____

_____

Building Critical Thinking

Using a five-paragraph essay consisting of an introductory paragraph, three body paragraphs, and one concluding paragraph, describe your experience why applying for college is a challenge to most students.

Prior to writing your essay, complete the outline below by stating three challenges you have faced. Refer to the *Study Notes* below for outlining.

Upon completing your essay, tear out a *Peer Feedback Form* in the back of the chapter, exchange your essay with someone in the group, and review his or her essay by providing constructive comments. Return the essay to your classmate.

Study Notes: Outlining a Longer Passage

- Writing an outline for a longer passage involves creating a thesis statement to form a visual structure that will help clarify your thoughts while writing.

- Each subsequent sentence within the body paragraph should support the thesis statement.

- Ties together the thesis statement with each detail into effective written work.

INSPIRATION

GRAMMAR PRACTICE VIA INTERNET

Go to one of the following websites:

- http://www.towson.edu/ows/sentencestruct.htm

- http://languagearts.pppst.com/sentencestructure.html

Research subjects and predicates and write the definition for each on the lines provided. Choose a sentence from the reading and identify the subject, the predicate verb, and object in the sentence. Underline the subject once, predicate verb twice, and circle the object.

_____

_____

_____

_____

_____

_____

_____

_____

CHAPTER 6: Immigration Stories, from Shadows to Spotlight

THE OUTLINE

I. Introduction

Thesis Statement – Main idea of your essay

_____

_____

_____

II. First Body Paragraph – First topic sentence to support your thesis statement

_____

_____

_____

Elaborate on your topic sentence

_____

_____

Provide an example/evidence/quotation

_____

Explain the significance of the example/evidence/quotation

_____

III. Second Body Paragraph – Second topic sentence to support your thesis statement

_____

_____

Elaborate on your topic sentence

_____

Provide an example/evidence/quotation

_____

Explain the significance of the example/evidence/quotation

_____

IV. Third Body Paragraph – Third topic sentence to support your thesis statement

_____

_____

Elaborate on your topic sentence

_____

Provide an example/evidence/quotation

_____

Explain the significance of the example/evidence/quotation

_____

V. Conclusion

Summarize your topic sentences. Discuss how the ideas in your three body paragraphs support your thesis statement.

_____

_____

_____

Peer Feedback Form

Written by: _____

Feedback by: _____

Date: _____

Title of the Essay: _____

1. What is the main point of this paper?

   _____

   _____

   _____

2. What are the supporting details of this paper?

   _____

   _____

   _____

3. What is an interesting or unique feature of this paper?

   _____

   _____

   _____

4. How could the writer improve this paper when he or she rewrites it? Make at least one suggestion.

   _____

   _____

   _____

Nutrition Facts

Serving Size ½ cup (114g)

Servings Per Container

Amount Per Serving		
	Calories from Fat 30	
Calories 90	% Daily Value	5%
		0%
Total Fat 3g		0%

unit 4

FOOD AND HEALTH

Image courtesy of the author.

Image courtesy of the author.

chapter 7
CITY MENU PUT ON DIET

PREREADING

Class Discussion

Discuss the following questions in a group.

1. What kind of junk food do you like? Why is it your favorite food?

   _____

   _____

   _____

2. What do the pictures on the next page remind you of?

   _____

   _____

   _____

3. Predict what the text will be about by reading the title.

   _____

   _____

   _____

Image courtesy of the author.

That's oil, Folks. New York is the first U.S. city to ban trans fats in restaurants.

Image courtesy of the author.

Dunkin' Donuts is investigating alternatives to trans fat oils to comply with the city's new code.

4. Predict what the text will be about by reading the first and last paragraphs (See pages 129-130).

_____

_____

5. Write how the author would develop the story.

_____

_____

Vocabulary in Context

Each item below includes a sentence from the reading. Using the context clues from this sentence, (1) determine the part of speech, and (2) formulate your own definition for the underlined word. Then (3) locate the word in a dictionary and write the appropriate definition.

1. "The Board of Health <u>unanimously</u> voted yesterday to make New York City the first municipality to ban artificial trans fats from restaurants and bakeries by July 2008." (Paragraph 1)

   (1) _____

   (2)_____

   (3)_____

2. "The Board of Health unanimously voted yesterday to make New York City the first <u>municipality</u> to ban artificial trans fats from restaurants and bakeries by July 2008." (1)

   (1) _____

   (2)_____

   (3)_____

3. "Chy's menu primarily consists of chicken, fish, and potatoes deep-fried in artery-<u>clogging</u> trans fat oils. (3)

    (1) _____

    (2)_____

    (3)_____

4. "While some <u>restaurateurs</u> applauded the moves, others said it might drive them out of business." (7)

    (1) _____

    (2)_____

    (3)_____

5. "While some restaurateurs <u>applauded</u> the moves, others said it might drive them out of business." (7)

    (1) _____

    (2)_____

    (3)_____

6. "In a statement yesterday, a Dunkin' Donuts spokeswoman said her company was 'actively investigating alternative oils to <u>eliminate</u> trans fats.'" (14)

    (1) _____

    (2)_____

    (3)_____

READING

CITY MENU PUT ON DIET

—Justin Rocket Silverman

The Rant: Tell us at amny.com/Rant if the trans fat ban is good for the city.

Get Outta Town
Here's a list of what amNewYork would like to see banned in the city:
1. Loud iPods on the subway
2. Cell phones in movie theaters
3. Ironic T-shirts
4. Pabst Blue Ribbon
5. Bedhead hair

[1]   The Board of Health unanimously voted yesterday to make New York City the first municipality to ban artificial trans fats from restaurants and bakeries by July 2008.

[2]   "To the rich people it doesn't matter," said Vanny Chy, owner of Chicken House on West 36th Street in Manhattan. "But for the poor people who can't afford more expensive food, they are going to suffer."

[3]   Chy's menu primarily consists of chicken, fish, and potatoes deep-fried in artery-clogging trans fat oils. He charges as little as $2.75 for fried fish, a price that he said would rise if he is forced to buy more expensive oils.

[4]   The city, however, said that the ban is designed to promote healthier eating and will not impact the "taste or availability of food."

[5]   Mayor Bloomberg said the changes could save lives. "We are trying to make food safer."

[6]   The city's health honchos also voted to require as many as 1 in 10 restaurants to begin listing the calorie content of their foods on the menu.

[7]   While some restaurateurs applauded the moves, others said it might drive them out of business. The New York State Restaurant Association is considering a court challenge to the ban.

[8]   "If a customer wants to know about the oil, I tell him. Why is the city telling me what my customers can eat?" Chy said. "But the city is the one carrying the guns, so what can I do?"

[9]   Postal worker Eddie Perez said he's been eating at the Chicken House for 18 years, and in all that time, they've only raised the price 50 cents. "If it goes up because of this health department ban, I think the place could be out of business," he lamented.

[10]   Restaurants have until July 1, 2007, to switch to a trans fat-free frying oil. Establishments that make their own baked goods have until July 1, 2008 to change.

[11]   Upscale restaurants such as The Four Seasons won't have a problem because their kitchens do not use trans fats, said Joel Patraker, purchasing manager for the dining landmark.

[12]   "We use a large amount of wonderful farm-fresh butter," he said. "For us ... it shouldn't be a problem at all. But if you are mass producing a line of products, it will take some re-tooling."

[13]   Fast food chains are experimenting with different frying oils to meet the city's deadline.

[14]   In a statement yesterday, a Dunkin' Donuts spokeswoman said her company was "actively investigating alternative oils to eliminate trans fats," and had already tested more than 20 oils. Contrary to rumors, she said, a "transformed" doughnut will not cost $3,000.

THE SKINNY ON TRANS FATS

—Mike Clancy

Luisa Borrell, an assistant professor in the epidemiology department at the Mailman School of Public Health at Columbia University, talks about trans fats.

Why are trans fats used?
They are supposed to enhance the taste and increase the shelf life of food.

Why are trans fats bad?
We have two kinds of cholesterol ... trans fats increase the low-density (bad) cholesterol, which causes cardiovascular disease.

What happens to your body when you eat food that contains trans fats?
You are only supposed to have between 2 and 2.5 grams of trans fat a day. ... If you have one doughnut, you are going to have between 8 and 12 grams of trans fat. If you do that every day, you are going to increase your cholesterol level and increase the fat plaque in your arteries. ... If it increases to the point where the blood cannot go through, that can lead to a stroke.

What do you think about the ban?
It's good for everybody, but the group that benefits the most are African Americans and Hispanics because they have the higher risk of cardiovascular disease. ... This will save at least 500 lives a year.

THE READING PROCESS

Topics, Main Ideas, and Details

1. What is the topic, or subject of this reading? Use the fewest words possible.

   _____

2. What is the main idea of this text? Underline it if directly stated. Write it in your own words if implied.

   _____

   _____

3. How is the main idea supported in the passage?

   _____

   _____

Identifying Details

Answer the following questions in complete sentences.

1. Why is trans fat bad? List one dangerous effect of trans fats to our health.

   _____

   _____

2. Why is trans fat used?

   _____

   _____

3. What deadline were restaurants given to transfer to non trans fat oils?

   _____

   _____

4. Why is trans fat being banned?

_____

_____

5. Why wouldn't upscale restaurants have a problem with the new law? Using information from the article, explain why this is so.

_____

_____

6. How many different oils did Dunkin' Donuts experiment with?

_____

_____

7. Who would benefit most from this ban?

_____

_____

Open-ended Questions

1. Which is the most important to you, the cost, calorie content, or flavor?

_____

_____

2. What other things would you like to see banned in the city besides items referred to in the article?

_____

_____

Drawing Inferences

The following information is not directly stated in the reading. Indicate whether the statement is true or false by writing T or F in the spaces provided.

_____ 1. Changing the city menus from trans fat to more expensive oils will not raise prices.

_____ 2. Restaurants keep information about food ingredients a secret.

_____ 3. Reworking the city menu is a challenging task.

_____ 4. Dunkin' Donuts is aggressively seeking to eliminate trans fat in their doughnuts.

_____ 5. Most people eat more than two and a half grams of trans fat a day.

Useful Words/Phrases

1. In the picture caption, the author uses a verb phrase *comply with*. What does this phrase mean? Write your own sentence by using this expression.

   _____

   _____

2. In Paragraph 14, the author uses *contrary to*. What does it mean? Write your own sentence by using this phrase.

   _____

   _____

Study Notes: Words That Signal Comparison Between Two Ideas

both	as
like	likewise
in the same way	similarly
alike	equally
as well as	in a similar fashion
in like manner	just as

INSPIRATION

Idiomatic Expressions

1. In Paragraph 3, what does it mean by *artery clogging*?

_____

_____

2. In Paragraph 8, what does it mean by *one carrying the guns, so what can I do*?

_____

_____

Vocabulary Practice

Match the underlined words with their definitions in the box. Write the appropriate answer letter in the spaces provided.

_____ 1. He worked endlessly to <u>promote</u> his new product.

_____ 2. The <u>honcho</u> of the group often bullied people.

_____ 3. The city council <u>unanimously</u> agreed to pass the law.

_____ 4. The drain was <u>clogged</u> by all the hair in the sink.

_____ 5. We have to come up with an <u>alternative</u> way to do this.

_____ 6. We must <u>comply</u> with the rules.

_____ 7. The <u>municipality</u> decided to change the law so it would be easier to abide by.

_____ 8. The <u>upscale</u> restaurant was the most popular place to eat in the city.

_____ 9. He began to <u>lament</u> the loss of his dog.

_____ 10. The human body has many <u>arteries</u>.

a.   the leader

b.   done in complete agreement

c.   a governing body of a district

d.   to block

e.   to help to exist or flourish

f.   the method that is not common or orthodox

g.   a blood vessel that carries blood away from the heart

h.   to act in accordance with

i.   to mourn

j.   high quality

POSTREADING

Reading Strategies

Read the questions below and answer in the spaces provided.

1. In reading this passage, what are you reminded of?

   Answer: This reading reminds me of _____

   _____

2. Were you satisfied with your prereading prediction about the text?

   Answer: I was/wasn't satisfied because _____

   _____

3. Do you have any questions about the reading?

   Answer: I wonder _____

   _____

4. What did you visualize while reading this passage?

   Answer: I visualized _____

   _____

5. Is this passage making sense to you?

   Answer: This passage is/isn't making sense to me because _____

   _____

6. What is the main idea of this reading?

   Answer: This reading is about _____

   _____

7. How can you relate the main idea to your own experiences?

   Answer: I can relate this passage to _____

   _____

8. Comment on the author's style of writing.

   Answer: When I read this passage, I feel _____

   _____

9. What have you learned?

   Answer: I have learned _____

   _____

10. During your reading of the text, what appeals to you that you'd like to try in your own writing?

    Answer: In my next writing I will try _____

    _____

Writing a Summary

Summarize the text in one paragraph, including (1) the title, author of the reading as well as the thesis statement; (2) significant details that support the main idea; and (3) restatement of the main idea in your own words. Note that the purpose of writing a summary is to accurately represent what the author wanted to say, not to provide a critique.

_____

_____

_____

_____

_____

_____

_____

_____

_____

APPLICATION

Internet Activities

1. Check out the U.S. Food and Drug Administration website at

    http://www.fda.gov

    Read the latest information concerning a dietary supplement. Write about its main points.

    _____

    _____

2. Go online and find out why trans fat is used. List two good purposes for trans fats.

    _____

    _____

    _____

3. Go online and find out who would benefit most from this ban. Write down your findings on the lines below.

    _____

    _____

4. Learn more about the New York City Department of Health and Mental Hygiene by clicking on

    http://www.nyc.gov/html/doh/html/home/home.shtml

    Write down one feature that appeals to you.

    _____

    _____

    _____

Reading-response Journal

List four high trans fat items and find substitutes for each. For example, French fries can be substituted by baked potato or baked potato chips.

_____

_____

_____

_____

_____

_____

_____

_____

_____

Building Critical Thinking

Using a five-paragraph essay consisting of an introductory paragraph, three body paragraphs, and one concluding paragraph, state three reasons why you would either support or oppose this ban on trans fat.

Prior to writing your essay, complete the outline in the back of the chapter by stating three arguments for and three arguments against this ban. Once you have selected a position, complete the essay.

Upon completing your essay, tear out a *Peer Feedback Form* in the back of the chapter, exchange your essay with someone in the group, and review his or her essay by providing constructive comments. Return the essay to your classmate.

GRAMMAR PRACTICE VIA INTERNET

Go to one of the following websites:

- http://www.ego4u.com/en/cram-up/grammar/conditional-sentences

- http://www.englishpage.com/conditional/conditionalintro.html

Research conditional sentences and write the definition. Identify a conditional sentence from the reading and explain its structure on the lines below.

_____

_____

_____

_____

_____

_____

_____

_____

_____

_____

_____

_____

_____

_____

_____

_____

FOLLOW-UP ARTICLE

STUDY: FAT BAN PAYING OFF

—Ivan Pereira

NYers eating better since city canned trans fats

[1]   A study released yesterday said that the mayor's trans fat ban has made New Yorkers healthier, and the nation show follow this lead.

[2]   Researchers found that between 2007 and 2009, New Yorkers consumed an average of 2.4 grams less of trans fats. The report, published in the Annals of Internal Medicine, was based on a five-year study into the city's eating habits at more than 160 fast food restaurants.

[3]   Christine Curtis, director of Nutrition Strategy for the city's Department of Health, which co-authored the report, said Mayor Michael Bloomberg's ban has not only made eateries offer healthier menus, but also inspired people to be more conscious of what they eat.

[4]   "This is great news for New Yorkers: restaurant food has less trans fat and everyone benefits," she said in a statement.

[5]   The report added that the federal government should consider following New York's lead and place restrictions on trans fat.

[6]   Maria Moriarty, a nutritionalist from Queens, agreed with the report's findings.

[7]   "I hear it from patients. They are more attuned to reading labels and they are happy when they see no trans fatty acids," she said.

THE OUTLINE
· ·

I. Introduction

Thesis Statement – Main idea of your essay

_____

_____

II. First Body Paragraph – First topic sentence to support your thesis statement

_____

_____

Elaborate on your topic sentence

_____

Provide an example/evidence/quotation

_____

Explain the significance of the example/evidence/quotation

_____

III. Second Body Paragraph – Second topic sentence to support your thesis statement

_____

_____

Elaborate on your topic sentence

_____

Provide an example/evidence/quotation

_____

Explain the significance of the example/evidence/quotation

_____

IV. Third Body Paragraph – Third topic sentence to support your thesis statement

_____

_____

Elaborate on your topic sentence

_____

Provide an example/evidence/quotation

_____

Explain the significance of the example/evidence/quotation

_____

V. Conclusion

Summarize your topic sentences. Discuss how the ideas in your three body paragraphs support your thesis statement.

_____

_____

_____

Peer Feedback Form

Written by: _____

Feedback by: _____

Date: _____

Title of the Essay: _____

1. What is the main point of this paper?

   _____

   _____

   _____

2. What are the supporting details of this paper?

   _____

   _____

   _____

3. What is an interesting or unique feature of this paper?

   _____

   _____

   _____

4. How could the writer improve this paper when he or she rewrites it? Make at least one suggestion.

   _____

   _____

   _____

chapter 8

SCHOOLS' TOUGHEST TEST: COOKING

PREREADING

Class Discussion

Discuss the following questions in a group.

1. Based on your experience, what kinds of food does your school cafeteria serve? List them.

_____

_____

_____

2. What do the pictures on the next page remind you of?

_____

_____

_____

3. Predict what the text will be about by reading the title.

_____

_____

_____

CHAPTER 8: Schools' Toughest Test: Cooking

4. Predict what the text will be about by reading the first and last paragraphs (See pages 147-152).

_____

_____

5. Write how the author would develop the story.

_____

_____

Vocabulary in Context

Each item below includes a sentence from the reading. Using the context clues from this sentence, (1) determine the part of speech, and (2) formulate your own definition for the underlined word. Then (3) locate the word in a dictionary and write the appropriate definition.

1. "Her job is to <u>entice</u> nearly 2,000 students at the height of adolescent squirreliness to eat a good lunch." (Paragraph 4)

   (1) _____

   (2)_____

   (3)_____

2. "She has to make curry from a limited list of <u>ingredients</u> approved by the Department of Education: frozen pre-roasted commodity chicken parts, jarred chopped garlic, and a generic curry power." (5)

   (1) _____

   (2)_____

   (3)_____

3. "Fresh chicken might improve it, but there isn't a <u>speck</u> of raw meat allowed in New York City school cafeterias." (6)

(1) _____

(2)_____

(3)_____

4. "It became cheaper to cull skilled kitchen labor, <u>eliminate</u> raw ingredients, and stop maintaining kitchens." (13)

(1) _____

(2)_____

(3)_____

5. "In a policy decision based on both need and efficiency, all the students get a free government-<u>subsidized</u> lunch." (24)

(1) _____

(2)_____

(3)_____

6. "Mrs. Barlatier <u>embraces</u> the mission like a cheery drill sergeant." (30)

(1) _____

(2)_____

(3)_____

7. "The curry recipe is a <u>compromise</u> between cooking with fresh ingredients and processed ones." (43)

(1) _____

(2)_____

(3)_____

CHAPTER 8: Schools' Toughest Test: Cooking

8. "She shut the deli bar, enduring shouts of protest and the kind of <u>incredulous</u> eye rolls that only a seventh-grade girl can deliver." (55)

(1) _____

(2)_____

(3)_____

READING

. . . .

SCHOOL'S TOUGHEST TEST: COOKING

—Kim Severson

[1]   On a recent Monday afternoon in the back of a middle school kitchen in Queens, it sounded as if a deal was going down.

[2]   "You want garam? I can get you garam."

[3]   Jorge Collazo, executive chef for New York City schools, was making an offer to Sharon Barlatier, the manager of one of the largest middle school cafeterias in New York, and, by extension, the country.

[4]   Her job is to entice nearly 2,000 students at the height of adolescent squir-reliness to eat a good lunch. Because many of her students at Middle School 137 come from families with Indian roots, curry is one of her secret weapons. The spice mix garam masala might improve its firepower.

[5]   She has to make curry from a limited list of ingredients approved by the Department of Education: frozen pre-roasted commodity chicken parts, jarred chopped garlic, and a generic curry powder.

[6]   Fresh chicken might improve it, but there isn't a speck of raw meat allowed in New York City school cafeterias. It poses too much of a food-handling challenge.

From <u>New York Times</u>, September 29, 2009, Dining In/Out Section, Section D, Page 1 by Kim Severson, New York Times Staff Writer. Copyright © 2009 by New York Times Company. Reprinted by permission.

[7]   So Mrs. Barlatier will settle for a little garam, even though Mr. Collazo will have to go out of his way to put it on the list.

[8]   Mrs. Barlatier is a rarity in a system that feeds almost a million children a day: she can cook, and she has the kitchen equipment to do it.

[9]   Many advocates for better, healthier school food have begun to believe that the only way to improve what students eat is to stop reheating processed food and start cooking real, fresh food.

[10]   But little actual cooking goes on in the nation's largest public school system, largely because little of it can. Barely half of New York's 1,385 school kitchens have enough cooking and fire-suppression equipment so cooks can actually sauté, brown, or boil over open flame.

[11]   Even in those that do, aging ovens sometimes don't heat properly, equipment is hidden away in storage rooms or broken, and the staff isn't trained to do much more than steam frozen vegetables, dig ravioli out of a six-pound can, or heat frozen chicken patties in a convection oven.

[12]   New York is not that unusual. More than 80 percent of the nation's districts cook fewer than half their entrees from scratch, according to a 2009 survey by the School Nutrition Association.

[13]   The slide didn't happen overnight. As many American families stopped cooking and began to rely on prepared and packaged food, so did the schools. It became cheaper to cut skilled kitchen labor, eliminate raw ingredients, and stop maintaining kitchens.

[14]   "In school food 30 or 40 years ago, they roasted turkeys and did all of these things," said Eric Goldstein, the chief executive of the Office of School Support Services.

[15]   "We all recognize we want to be scratch cooking again, but we have some challenges to get there."

[16]   Bill Telepan, the chef who runs the highly regarded restaurant Telepan on the Upper West Side, has been trying to get fresh food back into school kitchens

ever since he walked into his daughter's Manhattan elementary school a couple of years ago and found grape jelly and ketchup passing for barbecue sauce.

[17]   Through a program called Wellness in the Schools, started by a group of parents, he is reworking recipes and leading a team of culinary student volunteers who will work side by side with cooks in eight schools.

[18]   "The schools are like General Motors," Mr. Telepan said. "Over the years they created this cheap car that didn't last and they got burned. It can't last."

[19]   The fight for scratch cooking can feel like guerrilla warfare. In one Brooklyn elementary school, parents declared victory when they got the cooks to boil water and cook pasta.

[20]   M.S. 137 is one of the return-to-cooking strongholds, though it seems an improbable place for it.

[21]   The four-story school in Ozone Park is just down the street from a 24-hour White Castle and near two of the busiest streets in Queens. Although it opened in 2002, its halls are already crammed with hundreds more children than the school was designed for. Teachers without classrooms to call their own push carts full of materials from borrowed room to borrowed room.

[22]   Students wear only black and white clothes as a sort of uniform. Because there are no lockers, they haul around backpacks so full they look like turtles.

[23]   Class materials are translated into eight languages to accommodate students from Guyanese, Dominican and Bengali families. Only a few students come from the Italian families that used to fill the neighborhood.

[24]   And in a policy decision based on both need and efficiency, all the students get a free government-subsidized lunch. Still, the school has to make sure a certain number of children eat in order to receive the federal reimbursements.

[25]   The principal, Laura Mastrogiovanni, readily admits that food wasn't on her radar when she took over in 2005. The cafeteria keeps a separate budget and cooks don't report to her. But when Mrs. Barlatier arrived in 2007 and started to

improve the food, it didn't take long to see that the children not only ate more of it but seemed happier at lunch.

[26]   "They needed a little flair in their food," Mrs. Mastrogiovanni said. "It's good for their brains."

[27]   Like other newer schools in the city, M.S. 137 has a well-equipped kitchen. For schools around the country that aren't so lucky, $100 million in federal stimulus money was set aside this year for improvements.

[28]   Much of New York City's share of the money will buy nearly 100 salad bars, including 30-inchers low enough for elementary school students, as well as deli bars and refrigerators. It's not exactly fancy stoves and copper pots, but it is one more step toward serving fresh food.

[29]   But even with the best equipment in the world, you can't cook without cooks. So school officials use M.S. 137's large kitchen as a training center.

[30]   Mrs. Barlatier embraces the mission like a cheery drill sergeant. She pounds home the concept of kitchen organization in people for whom mise en place might as well be space shuttle repair. She empowers them to turn away produce orders filled with wilted parsley and moldy oranges and to use leftovers judiciously.

[31]   "If you would not eat it yourself, don't serve it," she admonishes.

[32]   She will not tolerate cooks who say students will eat only hamburgers or pizza or who complain that there is not enough equipment to cook the more complex recipes the district is trying to encourage.

[33]   "It's not the limit of the equipment," she tells them. "You can have only a steamer and make a sauce. You can have one burner and make a sauce. There is nothing stopping you."

[34]   Her remarkably tight-knit staff of 13 people put out an average of 1,400 meals between 11:09 a.m. and 2:06 p.m. The children come through the line in four shifts. That's like turning a 325-seat restaurant four times in three hours, except everyone is eating off foam trays and using those flimsy fork-spoon combinations called sporks.

[35]   It is a loud place, made even louder by the amplified voices of aides, who use microphones and whistles to keep everyone moving or sitting.

[36]   "No machines until you get your lunch!" an aide yells, trying to keep students from the bank of vending machines at the back of the cafeteria ringing with the siren call of Pop-Tarts and Cool Ranch Doritos.

[37]   The staff heats food in batches and regularly refreshes the well-stocked salad bar, which includes fresh coleslaw and potato salad made with oil and vinegar from mayonnaise-free recipes Mr. Collazo developed.

[38]   Still, Mrs. Barlatier does not get to cook what she wants. She has to turn out food like canned beef ravioli and sandwiches made with frozen chicken patties. The items are promised on the citywide menu. Leave them off and students might go home hungry and complain to their parents.

[39]   But she does get to play with special recipes to try and broaden the daily menus and appeal to the ethnic makeup of the students.

[40]   Mr. Collazo encourages that kind of cooking, but he is not convinced that everything has to be made from scratch.

[41]   "What's the advantage?" he said. Limited staff time and money is better spent creating fresher salad bars and preparing more interesting sauces for the pre-roasted chicken parts.

[42]   And he is quick to point out that school lunch has been improving in a thousand other small ways. The bread is whole wheat. The pasta is whole grain. Milk is low fat. The hamburgers, which arrive cooked and frozen, were once so lean and dry that cooks would simmer them in water to keep them moist. He found a company that made them more moist by adding textured vegetable protein to the ground beef. "Part of my job is to make sure the stuff that's getting heated in a box is decent and good," he said.

[43]   The curry recipe is a compromise between cooking with fresh ingredients and processed ones. It starts with frozen, cooked chicken parts that are left to defrost overnight, then heated in the morning.

[44]   Meanwhile, onions, green peppers, and celery are finely chopped and tossed with jarred garlic and oil into a 40-gallon tilted braising pan, the prized workhorse of the M.S. 137 kitchen.

[45]   Curry powder, chicken soup mix, pepper, and cumin are then stirred in, and the mixture is thickened with cornstarch before it is poured over the chicken.

[46]   "The kids love this curry," Mrs. Barlatier said. "It makes them feel comforted and cared for, which is what we want to do."

[47]   She promised a reporter that the children's enthusiasm for the curry would be easy to see. But there were early signs of trouble. Mrs. Barlatier had just introduced a deli bar. Two workers make custom sandwiches from a selection of freshly sliced cold cuts and cheeses.

[48]   Before the students reach the deli bar, they pass the curry station, which looked better than the buffet lines in a lot of Indian restaurants. There was a vegetarian version with peas and potatoes, and fluffy rice yellow with tumeric, garnished with a rose peeled from a tomato. And perhaps the biggest surprise? Chunks of plantains that came frozen but turned soft and sweet in the oven.

[49]   As the children began to pour in, Mrs. Barlatier ran back and forth in a long white coat, dispensing hugs and sporks.

[50]   The children come to treat her like a respected auntie by the end of the year. But on this day, she was about to become the mean lunch lady.

[51]   The lines were backing up. Some children might not have a chance to eat in the precious few minutes allotted them. The principal was becoming upset.

[52]   Mrs. Barlatier spotted the culprit: the deli bar. Students were passing on her lovely curry and waiting for their shot at custom-made sandwiches.

[53]   No matter how delicious her food is, she battles daily with the mercurial palate of the middle school student.

[54]   "You could have steak here and they are going for that deli," she said, exasperated.

[55]   It was time for action. She shut the deli bar, enduring shouts of protest and the kind of incredulous eye rolls that only a seventh-grade girl can deliver.

[56]   A sixth grader, asked why people were so crazy for what looked like a fairly unremarkable sandwich, explained.

[57]   "It's like Subway," he said, "but you don't have to pay."

THE READING PROCESS

Topics, Main Ideas, and Details

1. What is the topic, or subject of this reading? Use the fewest words possible.

   _____

2. What is the main idea of this text? Underline it if directly stated. Write it in your own words if implied.

   _____

   _____

3. How is the main idea supported in the passage?

   _____

   _____

Identifying Details

Answer the following questions in complete sentences.

1. Where is this test kitchen located? What makes it unique? Explain your answer.

   _____

   _____

2. Who is Mrs. Barlatier and what was her difficult task?

   _____

   _____

3. According to the text, what is the only way to improve what students eat?

_____

_____

4. In Paragraph 10, what does *it* refer to?

_____

_____

5. In Paragraph 13, what does it mean by *slide*?

_____

_____

6. What is wrong with the cafeteria food presently? What did Mrs. Barlatier do to change it?

_____

_____

7. Compare and contrast the way the test kitchen is currently running and what would be the ideal kitchen. Be sure to use a contrastive transitional word.

_____

_____

8. Define the kitchen at M.S. 137. List its characteristics.

_____

_____

9. How did the cooks protest when Mrs. Barlatier wanted to change the current kitchen system?

_____

_____

10. Who is Mr. Jorge Collazo? What is his position in improving New York City school cafeterias?

_____

_____

Open-ended Questions

Answer the following questions in complete sentences.

1. What are some challenges for a middle school cafeteria?

_____

_____

_____

2. What are Ms. Barlatier's roadblocks for cooking healthier school fare?

_____

_____

_____

Drawing Inferences

The following information is not directly stated in the reading. Indicate whether the statement is true or false by writing T or F in the spaces provided.

_____ 1. Many of the students at M.S. 137 come from immigrant families.

_____ 2. School kitchens are not allowed to cook over an open flame.

_____ 3. Many American families sit down at the dinner table every night.

_____ 4. School lunch programs are not well-monitored by Superintendents.

_____ 5. Mrs. Barlatier's attempt to feed students curry flavored food failed.

Useful Words/Phrases

1. In Paragraph 4, what does it mean by *secret weapons*?

   _____

   _____

2. In Paragraph 49, what does it mean by *pour in*?

   _____

   _____

Idiomatic Expressions

1. In Paragraph 1, what does it mean by *a deal was going down*?

   _____

   _____

2. In Paragraph 7, what does it mean by *go out of his way*?

   _____

   _____

Vocabulary Practice

A. Vocabulary Matching

Match the vocabulary words in Column A with their definitions in Column B, and write the correct letter in the spaces provided. Refer to the paragraph in the reading for context clues.

Column A		Column B
_____ 1. squirreliness (paragraph 4)		a. uncommon
_____ 2. generic	5	b. pasta filled with cheese or meat
_____ 3. commodity	5	c. universal
_____ 4. rarity	8	d. trim or adorn
_____ 5. ravioli	11	e. band of irregular soldiers
_____ 6. patties	11	f. main course
_____ 7. entrees	12	g. of the kitchen
_____ 8. scratch	15	h. a useful thing
_____ 9. culinary	17	i. correct
_____ 10. guerilla	19	j. sell
_____ 11. strongholds	20	k. without resourses
_____ 12. reimbursement	24	l. fortified place
_____ 13. admonish	31	m. picky
_____ 14. vend	36	n. pay back
_____ 15. garnish	48	o. small pie

B. Fill-in-the-Blanks

Choose one of the following words to best complete the sentences below. Some of the words were modified. Use each word only once. Be sure to pay close attention to the context clues provided.

advocate	accommodate	culprit	convince

1-2. The public _____ will admonish an adolescent if he is the _____ in an incredulous crime.

3-4. In an appeal to _____ the anxious bride, the wedding planner attempted to _____ her of a more decent dress.

compromise	embrace	exasperate	flimsy

5-6. College students _____ their abilities to cram for mid terms, usually to _____ their professors.

7-8. Do not _____ your character with _____ arguments or you will have to endure hardship.

amplify	broaden	commodity	empower

9-10. _____ your listening skills while you _____ your intelligence.

11-12. Take advantage of the _____ of time in your youth. Dispense with foolish living to _____ yourself with a productive life.

| batch | culinary | defrost | eliminate |

13-14. That _____ of cookies near the back burner will_____ if you need to make them for your dessert.

15-16. The _____ students use convection ovens over conventional ovens to _____ poor heat distribution when creating their prized ravioli dishes.

| firepower | ingredients | palate | subsidize |

17-18. The guerilla _____ was not enough to _____ the loss of the 9 soldiers which died in combat.

19-20. Many new restaurants attempt to entice its customers with fancy _____, garnish, and exotic flair to woo the mercurial _____ of a finicky client.

| braising | haul | lean | workhorse |

21-22. _____ a _____ patty of meat with melted cheese, onions and peppers creates a dish widely known as the Philly Cheese Steak.

23-24. Please _____ those heavy boxes judiciously otherwise your back will be not be able to tolerate the strain. Remember you are not a _____.

| generic | improbable | makeup | post |

25-26. The _____ _____ of some over the counter medicine is the same as those with a prescription.

27-28. The districts notice to delay its meeting was placed on a nearby _____ where it is _____ to be seen by its citizens.

declare	speck	moldy	simmer	tightknit

29-31. "I do _____", said the cook. A pound of _____ bread saved people's lives due to the _____ found known as penicillin.

32-33. The recipe for rice pudding requires that the flame be lowered to_____. The texture of the rice must become _____ almost jelly like and allowed to refrigerate overnight.

sauted	stronghold	suppress	translates

34-35. Olive oil mixed with butter _____, _____ a green, leafy vegetable like swiss chard into a delicious side dish.

36-37. In order to tear down a physical_____ in your life, you must readily exercise and _____ your urge to eat larger portions.

rarity	reimbursement	settle	vending

38-39. The lawyer encouraged his client to _____ the matter out of court so he could receive a more timely _____ to avoid the court fees.

40-41. A well-stocked _____ machine is a _____ at our lunch room cafeteria.

scratch	squirreliness

42-43. Food supplies were in such short supply during long winter months that the _____ of a pioneer woman would make you _____ your head in amazement.

POSTREADING

Reading Strategies

Read the questions below and answer in the spaces provided.

1. In reading this passage, what are you reminded of?

   Answer: This reading reminds me of _____

   _____

2. Were you satisfied with your prereading prediction about the text?

   Answer: I was/wasn't satisfied because _____

   _____

3. Do you have any questions about the reading?

   Answer: I wonder _____

   _____

4. What did you visualize while reading this passage?

   Answer: I visualized _____

   _____

5. Is this passage making sense to you?

   Answer: This passage is/isn't making sense to me because _____

   _____

6. What is the main idea of this reading?

   Answer: This reading is about _____

   _____

7. How can you relate the main idea to your own experiences?

Answer: I can relate this passage to _____

_____

8. Comment on the author's style of writing.

Answer: When I read this passage, I feel _____

_____

9. What have you learned?

Answer: I have learned _____

_____

10. During your reading of the text, what appeals to you that you'd like to try in your own writing?

Answer: In my next writing I will try _____

_____

Writing a Summary

Summarize the text in one paragraph, including (1) the title, author of the reading as well as the thesis statement; (2) significant details that support the main idea; and (3) restatement of the main idea in your own words. Note that the purpose of writing a summary is to accurately represent what the author wanted to say, not to provide a critique.

_____

_____

_____

_____

_____

_____

_____

_____

_____

APPLICATION . . . .

Internet Activities

1. Locate a public school in the town in which you currently live. Review the school's lunch menu, and list three healthy food choices and three less healthy food choices.

   Name of website: _____

   Web address: _____

   Food choices: _____

2. How does a student qualify for a free government-subsidized lunch? Go look it up and explore.

_____

_____

_____

Reading-response Journal

What food makes you feel comforted and cared for? Explain why.

_____

_____

_____

_____

_____

_____

_____

_____

_____

Building Critical Thinking

Imagine that you are the manager of your school cafeteria. Describe how you can make it better. List things that you'd like to change to improve the standards of your school cafeteria. Explain why.

Use a five-paragraph essay consisting of an introductory paragraph, three body paragraphs, and one concluding paragraph. Prior to writing your essay, complete the outline in the back of the chapter and then complete the essay.

Upon completing your essay, tear out a *Peer Feedback Form* in the back of the chapter, exchange your essay with someone in the group, and review his or her essay by providing constructive comments. Return the essay to your classmate.

GRAMMAR PRACTICE VIA INTERNET

Go to one of the following websites:

- http://www.towson.edu/ows/sentelmt.htm

- http://web.cn.edu/kwheeler/gram_clauses_n_phrases.html

Research what *phrases* are and write their definitions. Use information to refer back to reading for sentence structure containing *phrases*. Write down two sentences on the lines below and circle *phrases*.

_____

_____

_____

_____

_____

_____

_____

_____

_____

THE OUTLINE

I. Introduction

Thesis Statement – Main idea of your essay

_____

_____

II. First Body Paragraph – First topic sentence to support your thesis statement

_____

_____

Elaborate on your topic sentence

_____

Provide an example/evidence/quotation

_____

Explain the significance of the example/evidence/quotation

_____

III. Second Body Paragraph – Second topic sentence to support your thesis statement

_____

_____

Elaborate on your topic sentence

_____

Provide an example/evidence/quotation

_____

Explain the significance of the example/evidence/quotation

_____

IV. Third Body Paragraph – Third topic sentence to support your thesis statement

_____

_____

Elaborate on your topic sentence

_____

Provide an example/evidence/quotation

_____

Explain the significance of the example/evidence/quotation

_____

V. Conclusion

Summarize your topic sentences. Discuss how the ideas in your three body paragraphs support your thesis statement.

_____

_____

_____

Peer Feedback Form

Written by: _____

Feedback by: _____

Date: _____

Title of the Essay: _____

1. What is the main point of this paper?

   _____

   _____

   _____

2. What are the supporting details of this paper?

   _____

   _____

   _____

3. What is an interesting or unique feature of this paper?

   _____

   _____

   _____

4. How could the writer improve this paper when he or she rewrites it? Make at least one suggestion.

   _____

   _____

   _____

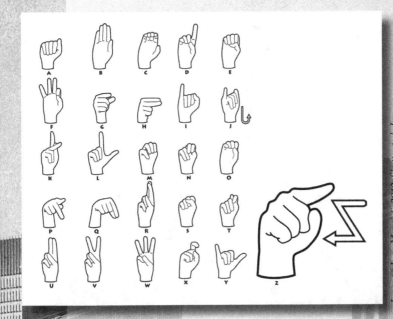

Image © Isaac Marzioli, 2012, Shutterstock, Inc.

unit 5
LANGUAGE ACQUISITION AND CLASSROOM INTERACTION

chapter 9

CHILDREN CONSTRUCT GRAMMARS

PREREADING

Class Discussion

Discuss the following questions in a group.

1. Do you speak any language(s) other than English? What are they?

   _____

   _____

   _____

2. What do the pictures on the next page remind you of?

   _____

   _____

   _____

3. Predict what the text will be about by reading the title.

   _____

   _____

   _____

CHAPTER 9: **Children Construct Grammars**

4. Predict what the text will be about by reading the first and last paragraphs (See pages 173-175).

_____

_____

5. Write how the author would develop the story.

_____

_____

Vocabulary in Context

Each item below includes a sentence from the reading. Using the context clues from this sentence, (1) determine the part of speech, and (2) formulate your own definition for the underlined word. Then (3) locate the word in a dictionary and write the appropriate definition.

1. "Children are not given <u>explicit</u> information about the rules, by either instruction or correction." (Paragraph 1)

   (1) _____

   (2) _____

   (3) _____

2. "Even deaf children of deaf signing parents go through stages in their signing development that <u>parallel</u> those of children acquiring spoken languages." (1)

   (1) _____

   (2) _____

   (3) _____

3. "Children do not produce questions by moving the first auxiliary. Instead, they correctly <u>invert</u> the auxiliary of the main clause." (4)

   (1) _____

   (2) _____

   (3) _____

4. "According to the innateness hypothesis, the child <u>extracts</u> from the linguistic environment those rules of grammar that are language specific, such as word order and movement rules." (9)

   (1) _____

   (2) _____

   (3) _____

5. "What accounts for the ease, rapidity, and uniformity of language acquisition in the face of <u>impoverished</u> data?" (10)

   (1) _____

   (2) _____

   (3) _____

6. "Because the child constructs his grammar according to an innate <u>blueprint</u>, all children proceed through similar developmental stages." (10)

   (1) _____

   (2) _____

   (3) _____

READING

. . . .

CHILDREN CONSTRUCT GRAMMARS

—Victoria Fromkin, Robert Rodman, and Nina Hyams

> We are designed to walk ... that we are taught to walk is impossible. And pretty much the same is true of language. Nobody is taught language. In fact, you can't prevent the child from learning it. (Noam Chomsky, The Human Language Series program 2, 1994.)

[1]   Language acquisition is a creative process. Children are not given explicit information about the rules, by either instruction or correction. They extract the rules of the grammar from the language they hear around them, and their linguistic environment does not need to be special in any way for them to do this. Observations of children acquiring different languages under different cultural and social circumstances reveal that the developmental stages are similar, possibly universal. Even deaf children of deaf signing parents go through stages in their signing development that parallel those of children acquiring spoken languages. These factors lead many linguists to believe that children are equipped with an innate template or blueprint for language—which we have referred to as Universal Grammar (UC)—and that this blueprint aids the child in the task of constructing a grammar for her language. This is referred to as the innateness hypothesis.

[2]   The innateness hypothesis receives its strongest support from the observation that the grammar a person ends up with is vastly underdetermined by his linguistic experience. In other words, we end up knowing far more about language than is exemplified in the language we hear around us. This argument for the innateness of UG is called the poverty of the stimulus.

[3]   Although children hear many utterances, the language they hear is incomplete, noisy, and unstructured. We said earlier that child-directed speech is largely well formed, but children are also exposed to adult-adult interactions. These utterances include slips of the tongue, false starts, ungrammatical and incomplete sentences, and no consistent information as to which utterances are well formed

From Fromkin/Rodman/Hyams. An Introduction to Language, 9/e. © 2011 Heinle/Arts & Sciences, a part of Cengage Learning, Inc. Reproduced by permission. www.cengage.com/permissions

and which are not. But most important is the fact that children come to know aspects of the grammar about which they receive **no** information. In this sense, the data they are exposed to is impoverished. It is less than what is necessary to account for the richness and complexity of the grammar they attain.

[4]   For example, we noted that the rules children construct are structure dependent. Children do not produce questions by moving the first auxiliary as in (1) below. Instead, they correctly invert the auxiliary of the main clause, as in (2). (We use _____, to mark the position from which a constituent moves.)

(1)   Is the boy who _____ sleeping is dreaming of a new car?

(2)   Is the boy who is sleeping _____ dreaming of a new car?

[5]   To come up with a rule that moves the auxiliary of the main clause rather than the first auxiliary, the child must know something about the structure of the sentence. Children are not told about structure dependency. They are not told about constituent structure. Indeed, adults who have not studied linguistics do not explicitly know about structure dependency, constituent structure, and other abstract properties of grammar and so could not instruct their children even if they were so inclined. This knowledge is tacit or implicit. The input children get is a sequence of sounds, not a set of phrase structure trees. No amount of imitation, reinforcement, analogy, or structured input will lead the child to formulate a phrase structure tree, much less a principle of structure dependency. Yet, children do create phrase structures, and the rules they acquire are sensitive to this structure.

[6]   The child must also learn many aspects of grammar from her specific linguistic environment. English-speaking children learn that the subject comes first and that the verb precedes the object inside the VP, that is, that English is an SVO language. Japanese children acquire an SOV language. They learn that the object precedes the verb.

[7]   English-speaking children must learn that yes-no questions are formed by moving the auxiliary to the beginning of the sentence, as follows:

You will come home. = Will you _____ come home?

[8]   Japanese children learn that to form a yes-no question, the morpheme –*ka* is suffixed to a verb stem.

   Tanaka ga sushi o tabete iru   "Tanaka is eating sushi."

   Tanaka ga sushi o tabete iruka   "Is Tanaka eating sushi?"

   In Japanese questions, sentence constituents are not rearranged.

[9]   According to the innateness hypothesis, the child extracts from the linguistic environment those rules of grammar that are language specific, such as word order and movement rules. But he does not need to learn universal principles like structure dependency, or general principles of sentence formation such as the fact that heads of categories can take complements. All these principles are part of the innate blueprint for language that children use to construct the grammar of their language.

[10]   The innateness hypothesis provides an answer to the logical problem of language acquisition posed by Chomsky: What accounts for the ease, rapidity, and uniformity of language acquisition in the face of improverished data? The answer is that children acquire a complex grammar quickly and easily without any particular help beyond exposure to the language because they do not start from scratch. UG provides them with a significant head start. It helps them to extract the rules of their language and to avoid many grammatical errors. Because the child constructs his grammar according to an innate blueprint, all children proceed through similar developmental stages.

[11]   The innateness hypothesis also predicts that all languages will conform to the principles of UG. We are still far from understanding the full nature of the principles of UG. Research on more languages provides a way to test any principles that linguists propose. If we investigate a language in which a posited UG principle is absent, we will have to correct our theory and substitute other principles, as scientists must do in any field. But there is little doubt that human languages conform to abstract universal principles and that the human brain is specially equipped for acquisition of human language grammars.

THE READING PROCESS

Topics, Main Ideas, and Details

1. What is the topic, or subject of this reading? Use the fewest words possible.

   _____

2. What is the main idea of this text? Underline it if directly stated. Write it in your own words if implied.

   _____

   _____

3. How is the main idea supported in the passage?

   _____

   _____

Identifying Details

Answer the following questions in complete sentences.

1. What is innateness hypothesis?

   _____

   _____

2. What is Universal Grammar?

   _____

   _____

3. In terms of progress, how do deaf children with parents that use sign language compare to children that can hear?

_____

_____

_____

4. What is poverty of the stimulus?

_____

_____

_____

5. How are adult-adult interactions detrimental to a child's grammatical development?

_____

_____

_____

6. How does a child develop his/her grammar?

_____

_____

_____

7. What is the logical problem of language acquisition?

_____

_____

_____

Relate to Yourself

1. Have you ever needed to speak another language to someone?

   _____

   _____

2. Do you feel that your language skills are sufficient for your academic needs?

   _____

   _____

   _____

Drawing Inferences

The following information is not directly stated in the reading. Indicate whether the statement is true or false by writing T or F in the spaces provided.

_____ 1. Children are highly exposed to correct instructions.

_____ 2. According to Noam Chomsky, children are born with some innateness to acquire grammars.

_____ 3. Noam Chomsky may agree that it is parents who teach their children grammars.

_____ 4. Due to parental language inconsistencies, children are encouraged to fill in the grammar gap.

Useful Words/Phrases

1. In Paragraph 1, what does it mean by *is referred to as*?

   _____

   _____

2. In Paragraphs 1 and 9, what is *blueprint*?

_____

_____

Idiomatic Expressions

1. In Paragraph 2, what is meant by *to end up with*?

_____

_____

2. In Paragraph 5, what does it mean by *to come up with*?

_____

_____

Vocabulary Practice

Fill-in-the-Blanks

Choose one of the following words to best complete the sentences below. Some of the words were modified. Use each word only once. Be sure to pay close attention to the context clues provided.

extract	reveal	explicit

1. He gave an _____ explanation to avoid questioning.

2. I managed to _____ the necessary information from the old man's ramblings.

3. After many years of research, the scientist was finally ready to _____ her findings.

equipped	template	parallel

4. If you are _____ with knowledge, you can do anything you want.

5. Many times, political parties share _____ ideas.

6. If you follow a _____ you will be better organized.

blueprints	utterances	attained

7. Many years have passed and I still haven't _____ my goals.

8. _____ are needed to know what to do in architecture.

9. The _____ of the sailors were crude and impolite.

tacit	impoverished	auxiliary

10. No matter how hard some try, they cannot understand a _____ approach.

11. In case the main supplies run out, we have our _____ supplies.

12. After the crushing loss, the team's spirit felt _____.

inclined	invert	conform

13. When the password code was incorrect, I tried to _____ it.

14. After the debate, he was _____ to give in.

15. We must _____ to the laws without question.

formulating	implicit

16. _____ a plan is the first step to action.

17. Sarcasm is often an _____ insult.

POSTREADING

Reading Strategies

Read the questions below and answer in the spaces provided.

1. In reading this passage, what are you reminded of?

   Answer: This reading reminds me of _____

   _____

2. Were you satisfied with your prereading prediction about the text?

   Answer: I was/wasn't satisfied because _____

   _____

3. Do you have any questions about the reading?

   Answer: I wonder _____

   _____

4. What did you visualize while reading this passage?

   Answer: I visualized _____

   _____

5. Is this passage making sense to you?

   Answer: This passage is/isn't making sense to me because _____

   _____

6. What is the main idea of this reading?

   Answer: This reading is about _____

   _____

7. How can you relate the main idea to your own experiences?

   Answer: I can relate this passage to _____

   _____

8. Comment on the author's style of writing.

   Answer: When I read this passage, I feel _____

   _____

9. What have you learned?

   Answer: I have learned _____

   _____

10. During your reading of the text, what appeals to you that you'd like to try in your own writing?

    Answer: In my next writing I will try _____

    _____

Writing a Summary

Summarize the text in one paragraph, including (1) the title, author of the reading as well as the thesis statement; (2) significant details that support the main idea; and (3) restatement of the main idea in your own words. Note that the purpose of writing a summary is to accurately represent what the author wanted to say, not to provide a critique.

_____

_____

_____

_____

_____

_____

_____

_____

APPLICATION

Internet Activities

1. Find out who Noam Chomsky is. Share your findings with your classmates.

_____

_____

2. Create a sentence and translate it into another language of your choice.

   www.babelfish.com

   _____

   _____

Reading-response Journal

Listen to a young child's speech under 5, either in real life or on TV. Document your observations.

_____

_____

_____

_____

_____

_____

_____

_____

_____

CHAPTER 9: Children Construct Grammars

Building Critical Thinking

Using a five-paragraph essay consisting of an introductory paragraph, three body paragraphs, and one concluding paragraph, describe what aids you to develop your language skills.

Prior to writing your essay, complete the outline in the back of the chapter and then complete the essay.

Upon completing your essay, tear out a *Peer Feedback Form* in the back of the chapter, exchange your essay with someone in the group, and review his or her essay by providing constructive comments. Return the essay to your classmate.

GRAMMAR PRACTICE VIA INTERNET

Go to one of the following websites:

- http://writingcenter.unc.edu/resources/handouts-demos/citation/passive-voice

- http://grammar.ccc.commnet.edu/grammar/passive.htm

Research the passive voice and write the definition. Identify a sentence that contains the passive voice from the reading and explain its structure on the lines below.

_____

_____

_____

_____

_____

_____

_____

_____

THE OUTLINE
· ·

I. Introduction

Thesis Statement – Main idea of your essay

_____

_____

II. First Body Paragraph – First topic sentence to support your thesis statement

_____

_____

Elaborate on your topic sentence

_____

Provide an example/evidence/quotation

_____

Explain the significance of the example/evidence/quotation

_____

III. Second Body Paragraph – Second topic sentence to support your thesis statement

_____

_____

Elaborate on your topic sentence

_____

Provide an example/evidence/quotation

_____

Explain the significance of the example/evidence/quotation

_____

IV. Third Body Paragraph – Third topic sentence to support your thesis statement

_____

_____

Elaborate on your topic sentence

_____

Provide an example/evidence/quotation

_____

Explain the significance of the example/evidence/quotation

_____

V. Conclusion

Summarize your topic sentences. Discuss how the ideas in your three body paragraphs support your thesis statement.

_____

_____

_____

Peer Feedback Form

Written by: _____

Feedback by: _____

Date: _____

Title of the Essay: _____

1. What is the main point of this paper?

   _____

   _____

   _____

2. What are the supporting details of this paper?

   _____

   _____

   _____

3. What is an interesting or unique feature of this paper?

   _____

   _____

   _____

4. How could the writer improve this paper when he or she rewrites it? Make at least one suggestion.

   _____

   _____

   _____

chapter 10

RAPPORT-BUILDING DEVICES IN A TEACHER-STUDENT INTERACTION

PREREADING

Class Discussion

Discuss the following questions in a group.

1. Who was your best teacher? Describe him/her.

_____

_____

_____

2. What do the pictures on the next page remind you of?

_____

_____

_____

3. Predict what the text will be about by reading the title.

_____

_____

_____

Image © auremar, 2012. Shutterstock, Inc.

Image © Dmitry Nikolaev, 2012. Shutterstock, Inc.

CHAPTER 10: Rapport-building Devices in a Teacher-student Interaction

4. Predict what the text will be about by reading the first and last paragraphs (See pages 191-193).

_____

_____

5. Write how the author would develop the story.

_____

_____

Vocabulary in Context

Each item below includes a sentence from the reading. Using the context clues from this sentence, (1) determine the part of speech, and (2) formulate your own definition for the underlined word. Then (3) locate the word in a dictionary and write the appropriate definition.

1. "This responsiveness to another's influence is the key factor in the <u>notion</u> of the term rapport." (Paragraph 1)

   (1) _____

   (2) _____

   (3)_____

2. "According to their research, greater <u>opportunities</u> for rapport to develop occur in focused interactions, when participants cooperate to maintain a single focused interaction through communication with one another." (2)

   (1) _____

   (2) _____

   (3)_____

3. "Furthermore, the correlations reveal that nonverbal immediacy is more highly correlated with learning than verbal immediacy." (4)

    (1) _____

    (2) _____

    (3)_____

4. "Then, the participants were asked to select from a list of specific behaviors which characterized those teachers." (5)

    (1) _____

    (2) _____

    (3)_____

5. "A total of 952 college students participated in a survey concerning teacher immediacy and perceived cognitive, affective, and behavioral learning." (6)

    (1) _____

    (2) _____

    (3)_____

6. "A number of studies have suggested that immediacy behaviors which signal approach, openness for communication, and warmth enhance teacher-student relationships and potentially student learning." (7)

    (1) _____

    (2) _____

    (3)_____

READING

. . . .

RAPPORT-BUILDING DEVICES IN A TEACHER-STUDENT INTERACTION[1]

—Anna H.-J. Do

[1]   When people are engaged in interaction, they would likely listen to, be responsive to, and be influenced by individuals with whom they feel they are communicating. This responsiveness to another's influence is the key factor in the notion of the term rapport. Rapport has been studied in a variety of ways and relates to such conversational phenomena as conversational involvement, engagement, or adjustment.

[2]   In an attempt to define group rapport related to nonverbal behavior, Tickle-Degnen and Rosenthal (1987) approached rapport as an aspect of the interaction among participants who are engaged in a conversation. They also describe rapport as a quality evident in certain relationships. According to their research, greater opportunities for rapport to develop occur in focused interactions, when participants cooperate to maintain a single focused interaction through communication with one another. They present three essential components of rapport: mutual attention and involvement, positivity, and coordination.

[3]   With respect to the relationship between nonverbal behavior and group rapport, they find that nonverbal behavior seems to be a correlate of three elements mentioned above, to function as an antecedent to feelings and ratings of rapport. Tickle-Degnen and Rosenthal further elaborate that behaviors of mutual attention enhance feelings of mutual interest; positive behaviors are connected to feelings of friendliness and warmth; and coordinated interactional behaviors are related to feelings of balance and harmony.

[4]   Christophel (1990) explored the importance of teacher-student rapport by looking into learner outcomes. In an attempt to determine perception of teacher immediacy (i.e., degree of perceived physical and/or psychological closeness

---

1 This article is based on the author's unpublished Master's research paper entitled, "Group Rapport-Building Devices in an Institutionalized Face-to-face Interaction," submitted to Georgetown University.

between people) to student motivation and their combined impact on learning outcomes, Christophel recruited graduate and undergraduate students, teaching assistants, and faculty from a wide range of university classes. Self-report measures of teachers' behavior, adopted by Gorham (1988), were given to the subjects they attend. The results point out that student perceptions of teacher verbal and nonverbal immediacy behaviors such as vocal expressiveness, eye contact, gestures, smiling, and a relaxed body position are positively associated with the students' motivation and with their perceptions of their own learning. Furthermore, the correlations reveal that nonverbal immediacy is more highly correlated with learning than verbal immediacy. These verbal and nonverbal behaviors which contribute to the outcome of the interaction are crucial ingredients in developing and maintaining rapport.

[5]   Gorham (1988) specifically examined student perceptions of teacher verbal immediacy behaviors associated with learning. Forty-seven undergraduate students enrolled in basic, non-required communication courses participated in a small-group brainstorming exercise in which they were asked to think of the best teachers they ever had. Then, the participants were asked to select from a list of specific behaviors which characterized those teachers. The list included 20 verbal behaviors followed by 14 nonverbal behaviors (adopted by Richmond, Gorham, and McCroskey [1987]) which were identified as immediacy behaviors. The subjects indicated that the teachers' verbal as well as nonverbal behaviors determined what teachers the students remembered as being their best teachers. The teacher's use of humor, praise of students' work, actions, or comments, and frequency of initiating and/or willingness to be engaged in conversations before, after, or outside of class were particularly significant verbal immediacy cues. Students also identified the following teacher behaviors: (1) self-disclosure; (2) asking questions or encouraging students to talk; (3) asking questions that solicit viewpoints or opinions; (4) following up on student-initiated topics; (5) reference to class as "our" class; (6) asking how students feel about assignments, due dates or discussion topics; and (7) invitations for students to telephone or meet with him/her outside of class. Nonverbal behaviors, such as vocal expressiveness, smiling, relaxed body position, gestures, eye contact, movement around the classroom, and touch were found to be nonverbal immediacy cues that significantly related to students' perceptions of good teachers. Both sets of behaviors are associated with notions of rapport.

[6]   A study by Sanders and Wiseman (1990) reinforces the findings of the Gorham study. In the Sanders and Wiseman study, based on the multicultural classrooms (White, Asian, Hispanic, Black), a total of 952 college students participated in a survey concerning teacher immediacy and perceived cognitive, affective, and behavioral learning. By using modified versions of Richmond, Gorham, and McCroskey's (1987) nonverbal behavior index and Gorham's (1988) verbal immediacy behavior scale, they found that teacher immediacy was positively associated with learning for all groups, regardless of ethnicity although the levels of association vary. This suggests that teacher immediacy creates a supportive learning environment for the class.

[7]   In summation, a number of studies have suggested that immediacy behaviors which signal approach, openness for communication, and warmth enhance teacher-student relationships and potentially student learning. Although group rapport seems to be effective in teaching in terms of involving students in classroom interaction, it is necessary for the teachers to adjust to each student's sensitivity and the dynamics of each classroom. The results also depend on *how* teachers use group rapport-building devices, that is, a good way to establish group rapport for one teacher may not always be good for another. Some teachers attempt to build group rapport by having less distance with their students, whereas others may assert more authority in a way that works for them. Therefore, it is important to consider the variables of students such as gender, age, personality, and cultural background and so forth.

THE READING PROCESS

Topics, Main Ideas, and Details

1. What is the topic, or subject of this reading? Use the fewest words possible.

   _____

2. What is the main idea of this text? Underline it if directly stated. Write it in your own words if implied.

_____

_____

3. How is the main idea supported in the passage?

_____

_____

Identifying Details

1. Why is the term *rapport* important in this article?

_____

_____

2. According to Tickle-Degnen and Rosenthal, what are the three crucial components of rapport?

_____

_____

3. What did Tickle-Degnen and Rosenthal find about the relationship between nonverbal behavior and group rapport?

_____

_____

4. Whose study did Christophel modify?

_____

_____

5. What are Christophel's findings?

_____

_____

6. What was the purpose of Gorham's (1988) study?

_____

_____

7. According to Gorham, what are the examples of verbal immediacy behaviors? List only four.

_____

_____

8. According to Gorham, what are the examples of nonverbal immediacy behaviors? List only four.

_____

_____

9. What is one feature that is unique to Sanders and Wiseman's (1990) study in terms of their subjects?

_____

_____

10. What are Sanders and Wiseman's (1990) findings?

_____

_____

Open-ended Questions

1. What was the author's purpose in writing this article?

    _____

    _____

    _____

2. Do you believe there is validity in this article?

    _____

    _____

    _____

3. Discuss some features of one of your best teachers.

    _____

    _____

    _____

Drawing Inferences

The following information is not directly stated in the reading. Indicate whether the statement is true or false by writing T or F in the spaces provided.

_____ 1. Building student-teacher rapport comes by signing up for the class.

_____ 2. According to Tickle-Degnen and Rosenthal, rapport develops when everyone is communicating about the same topic.

_____ 3. Nonverbal communication has no place in building rapport.

_____ 4. Teacher immediacy works regardless of ethnicity.

Useful Words/Phrases

1. In Paragraph 1, the author uses a phrase *key factor*. What does it mean? Use this phrase in a sentence.

_____

_____

_____

2. In Paragraph 7, the author begins the paragraph by *in summation*. What does it mean? What is its function?

_____

_____

_____

Idiomatic Expressions

1. In Paragraph 3, what does *with respect to* mean? Write your own sentence by using this phrase.

_____

_____

2. In Paragraph 4, what is *point out*? Use this phrase in a sentence.

_____

_____

Vocabulary Practice

Fill-in-the-Blanks

Choose one of the following words to best complete the sentences below. Some of the words were modified. Use each word only once. Be sure to pay close attention to the context clues provided.

enhancing	mutually	rapport

1. A _____ between student and teacher is built by mutual attention and involvement.

2. We met for lunch at a _____ agreed-upon restaurant.

3. Salt and pepper are key ingredients used when _____ the flavor of beef.

engaged	correlation	phenomena

4. Many studies have found that there is a _____ between group rapport and student learning.

5. To be fully _____ in a conversation, you must be a good listener.

6. It is a _____ when children pick up after themselves.

elaborate	recruited	crucial

7. The jurors ask each witness to _____ on his testimonies.

8. The sergeant _____ cadets for working the midnight outposts.

9. Working fire alarms are _____ elements in obtaining a certificate at the time of a house sale.

reinforced	antecedent	outcomes

10. In developing a behavior modification plan, you must consider the _____ which triggered the negative behavior.

11. We try very hard to control the _____ of daily situations.

12. Rules of behavior need to be _____ at home.

solicitation	disclosure

13. Many people are uncomfortable providing a full _____ of their tax statements.

14. It is the bookstore policy to prohibit _____ of certain literature.

POSTREADING

. . . .

Reading Strategies

Read the questions below and answer in the spaces provided.

1. In reading this passage, what are you reminded of?

   Answer: This reading reminds me of _____

   _____

2. Were you satisfied with your prereading prediction about the text?

   Answer: I was/wasn't satisfied because _____

   _____

3. Do you have any questions about the reading?

   Answer: I wonder _____

   _____

4. What did you visualize while reading this passage?

   Answer: I visualized _____

   _____

5. Is this passage making sense to you?

   Answer: This passage is/isn't making sense to me because _____

   _____

6. What is the main idea of this reading?

   Answer: This reading is about _____

   _____

7. How can you relate the main idea to your own experiences?

   Answer: I can relate this passage to _____

   _____

8. Comment on the author's style of writing.

   Answer: When I read this passage, I feel _____

   _____

9. What have you learned?

   Answer: I have learned _____

   _____

10. During your reading of the text, what appeals to you that you'd like to try in your own writing?

Answer: In my next writing I will try _____

_____

Writing a Summary

Summarize the text in one paragraph, including (1) the title, author of the reading as well as the thesis statement; (2) significant details that support the main idea; and (3) restatement of the main idea in your own words. Note that the purpose of writing a summary is to accurately represent what the author wanted to say, not to provide a critique.

_____

_____

_____

_____

_____

_____

_____

_____

_____

_____

_____

_____

_____

APPLICATION

Internet Activity

Go to psychologicalandscience.org/teaching/tips and read more about rapport building between teacher and student. List four components that are addressed in this article.

_____

_____

_____

_____

_____

Reading-response Journal

Should teachers become friends with their students? What are the boundaries of this relationship?

_____

_____

_____

_____

_____

_____

_____

_____

Building Critical Thinking

In your face-to-face interaction with your professors, do you feel building a sense of rapport helps you learn your material better? What are the rapport-building devices that help you learn better?

Using a five-paragraph essay consisting of an introductory paragraph, three body paragraphs, and one concluding paragraph, state three rapport-building devices that would help your learning.

Prior to writing your essay, complete the outline in the back of the chapter and then complete the essay.

Upon completing your essay, tear out a *Peer Feedback Form* in the back of the chapter, exchange your essay with someone in the group, and review his or her essay by providing constructive comments. Return the essay to your classmate.

GRAMMAR PRACTICE VIA INTERNET

Go to one of the following websites:

- http://grammar.ccc.commnet.edu/grammar/prepositions.htm

- http://www.chompchomp.com/terms/preposition.htm

- http://www.better-english.com/grammar/prepositions.htm

Research prepositions and write their definitions. Identify sentences that contain prepositions from the reading and explain their structures on the lines below.

_____

_____

_____

_____

_____

THE OUTLINE

I. Introduction

Thesis Statement – Main idea of your essay

_____

_____

II. First Body Paragraph – First topic sentence to support your thesis statement

_____

_____

Elaborate on your topic sentence

_____

Provide an example/evidence/quotation

_____

Explain the significance of the example/evidence/quotation

_____

III. Second Body Paragraph – Second topic sentence to support your thesis statement

_____

_____

Elaborate on your topic sentence

_____

Provide an example/evidence/quotation

_____

Explain the significance of the example/evidence/quotation

_____

IV. Third Body Paragraph – Third topic sentence to support your thesis statement

_____

_____

Elaborate on your topic sentence

_____

Provide an example/evidence/quotation

_____

Explain the significance of the example/evidence/quotation

_____

V. Conclusion

Summarize your topic sentences. Discuss how the ideas in your three body paragraphs support your thesis statement.

_____

_____

_____

Peer Feedback Form

Written by: _____

Feedback by: _____

Date: _____

Title of the Essay: _____

1. What is the main point of this paper?

   _____

   _____

   _____

2. What are the supporting details of this paper?

   _____

   _____

   _____

3. What is an interesting or unique feature of this paper?

   _____

   _____

   _____

4. How could the writer improve this paper when he or she rewrites it? Make at least one suggestion.

   _____

   _____

   _____

unit 6

TECHNOLOGY

chapter 11

TECH TARGETS

PREREADING
. . . .

Class Discussion

Discuss the following questions in a group.

1. Do you use an iPod? What does it do for you?

   _____

   _____

   _____

2. What do the pictures on the next page remind you of?

   _____

   _____

   _____

3. Predict what the text will be about by reading the title.

   _____

   _____

   _____

Image © tsaplia, 2012. Shutterstock, Inc.

170: Pedestrian fatalities in the city in 2006

Image © Bridget Zawitoski, 2012. Shutterstock, Inc.

Proposed state legislation would fine pedestrians who cross the street while using their iPods.

4. Predict what the text will be about by reading the first and last paragraphs (See pages 211-212).

_____

_____

5. Write how the author would develop the story.

_____

_____

Vocabulary in Context

Each item below includes a sentence from the reading. Using the context clues from this sentence, (1) determine the part of speech, and (2) formulate your own definition for the underlined word/phrase. Then (3) locate the word in a dictionary and write the appropriate definition.

1. "Spaced-out pedestrians should get fines, says pol." (Subtitle)

    (1) _____

    (2)_____

    (3)_____

2. "You can't be fully aware of your surroundings if you're fiddling with a BlackBerry, dialing a phone number, playing 'Super Mario Brothers' on a Game Boy or listening to music on an iPod,' Kruger said." (5)

    (1) _____

    (2)_____

    (3)_____

3. "He said the legislation will save lives, noting a recent spate of fatal accidents involving pedestrians wearing headphones." (6)

    (1) _____

    (2)_____

    (3)_____

4. "iPods and Walkmans don't kill pedestrians, <u>reckless</u> driving kills pedestrians." (11)

   (1) _____

   (2) _____

   (3) _____

5. "B'klyn pol not the first to <u>give walkers an earful</u>." (Subtitle)

   (1) _____

   (2) _____

   (3) _____

6. "Sen. Carl Kruger's proposed ban on iPods for street-crossing pedestrians isn't <u>making music history</u>." (Box)

   (1) _____

   (2) _____

   (3) _____

READING

. . . .

TECH TARGETS

—James Fanelli

Spaced-out pedestrians should get fines, says pol

[1]   They're the inevitable street encounters in a metropolis tethered to its portable electronic devices: the meandering businessman typing a text message on

his BlackBerry, the chatty cell phone user coming to a dead stop on a crowded sidewalk, and the iPod listener obliviously crossing a street as the light changes.

[2]   Technology has allowed New Yorkers to go mobile with their media, but it has also put their legs on automatic pilot while they tune into games, e-mail, and music.

[3]   Now one lawmaker wants to put an end to this habit of modern life.

[4]   New legislation proposed by state Sen. Carl Kruger (D-Brooklyn) would fine pedestrians and bicyclists if they use their iPod, cell phone, or other PDA while crossing a city street.

[5]   "You can't be fully aware of your surroundings if you're fiddling with a Black-Berry, dialing a phone number, playing 'Super Mario Brothers' on a Game Boy, or listening to music on an iPod," Kruger said.

[6]   He said the legislation will save lives, noting a recent spate of fatal accidents involving pedestrians wearing headphones.

[7]   Under the legislation, anyone crossing the street while using an electronic device would be issued a court summons that carries a $100 penalty.

[8]   New Yorkers yesterday said that electronic devices have become distractions.

[9]   "It's a problem usually when people are crossing the street," said Shawn Mullins, 21, of Flushing. "It happened to my friend the other day. He was talking on his cell phone and looking the other way, and some guy came zooming by and almost hit him."

[10]   City advocacy group Transportation Alternatives, however, called the proposal misguided because it targets the wrong people.

[11]   "It's blaming the victim," said Paul Steely White, the group's executive director. "iPods and Walkmans don't kill pedestrians, reckless driving kills pedestrians."

B'klyn pol not the first to give walkers an earful

Sen. Carl Kruger's proposed ban on iPods for street-crossing pedestrians isn't making music history.

Back in 1982, in the heyday of a less-sophisticated portable music player, the Sony Walkman, a New Jersey township proposed an ordinance similar to the Brooklyn lawmaker's, The New York Times reported.

Woodbridge, N.J., officials wanted to make it illegal to wear headphones while crossing the street. The ordinance would have fined lawbreakers $50.

Word on the Street
Are people too caught up in their electronic devices?
"Today you can spend a whole day without meeting anyone else. It's more common to hear the intimate details of someone's conversation than it is to actually say hello to them. " - Kevin Arbouet, 29, New York
"I see a lot of people that don't pay attention to traffic. I've seen people come close to getting hit. People aren't paying attention to what they're doing. - Diego Ponce, 32, Kew Gardens
"I've seen people while they're eating with others, talking on their cell phones and not paying attention to the people they're with." - Kim Sanders, 19, New Hyde Park

THE READING PROCESS

Topics, Main Ideas, and Details

1. What is the topic, or subject of this reading? Use the fewest words possible.

   _____

2. What is the main idea of this text? Underline it if directly stated. Write it in your own words if implied.

   _____

   _____

3. How is the main idea supported in the passage?

   _____

   _____

Identifying Details

Answer the following questions in complete sentences.

1. Why has technology become a problem in the busy streets of New York City?

   _____

   _____

   _____

2. What does the new legislation propose?

   _____

   _____

   _____

3. What called attention to the use of electronics by pedestrians?

   _____

   _____

   _____

4. How much is the fine?

   _____

5. What did Paul Steely White say in defense of the use of electronics on city streets?

   _____

   _____

   _____

6. Who proposed the ban of electronics in New York City?

   _____

Open-ended Questions

1. What was the author's purpose in writing this article?

   _____

   _____

   _____

2. Would you go to court or pay the fine if you receive the ticket for wearing headphones while crossing city streets?

   _____

   _____

   _____

3. Do you think people are too caught up in their electronic devices?

   _____

   _____

   _____

Drawing Inferences

The following information is not directly stated in the reading. Indicate whether the statement is true or false by writing T or F in the spaces provided.

_____ 1. According to the law, pedestrians have the right to use cell phones and iPods.

_____ 2. Senator Carl Kruger is the first politician to put a ban on wearing headphones.

_____ 3. We have become a society of multi-taskers.

_____ 4. Even young people feel that using cell phones in social interactions is acceptable.

Useful Words/Phrases

1. In Paragraph 1, what is a *metropolis*? Use the word in a sentence.

   _____

   _____

2. In Paragraph 10, what is *misguided*? Use the word in a sentence.

   _____

   _____

Idiomatic Expressions

1. In Paragraph 1, what is *coming to a dead stop*?

   _____

   _____

2. In Paragraph 2, what is *put their legs on automatic pilot*?

   _____

   _____

Vocabulary Practice

Match the underlined words with their definitions in the box. Write the appropriate answer letter in the spaces provided.

_____ 1. Taxes and death are <u>inevitable</u> events in our lives.

_____ 2. On the way to the campgrounds, we <u>encountered</u> a bear.

_____ 3. Many of the students were <u>tethered</u> by their excessive school work.

_____ 4. In war, it is almost impossible to avoid <u>fatalities.</u>

_____ 5. The homeless man spent his days <u>meandering</u> along the streets of the busy city.

_____ 6. He was <u>spaced-out</u> in front of the whole class.

_____ 7. She spent her days <u>fiddling</u> with various gadgets she amassed over the years.

_____ 8. When she heard the bad news, she went on a tantrum due to a <u>spate</u> of anger.

_____ 9. His rather <u>reckless</u> demeanor often got him in trouble.

_____ 10. Since he <u>obliviously</u> crossed the street, he almost got hit by a car.

_____ 11. The town <u>ordinance</u> banned excessive noise after 10 o'clock p.m.

---

a. to meet unexpectedly

b. death due to an occurrence

c. something that is bound to happen

d. to wander aimlessly

e. being tied up or occupied

f. to touch or manipulate something as to operate or adjust it

g. utterly unconcerned about the consequences of some action; without caution

h. distracted or a trance-like state

i. to do without any thought or consideration of outside stimuli

j. a sudden, almost overwhelming, outpouring

k. a public regulation

POSTREADING

Reading Strategies

Read the questions on the next page and answer in the spaces provided.

1. In reading this passage, what are you reminded of?

   Answer: This reading reminds me of _____

   _____

2. Were you satisfied with your prereading prediction about the text?

   Answer: I was/wasn't satisfied because _____

   _____

3. Do you have any questions about the reading?

   Answer: I wonder _____

   _____

4. What did you visualize while reading this passage?

   Answer: I visualized _____

   _____

5. Is this passage making sense to you?

   Answer: This passage is/isn't making sense to me because _____

   _____

6. What is the main idea of this reading?

   Answer: This reading is about _____

   _____

7. How can you relate the main idea to your own experiences?

   Answer: I can relate this passage to _____

   _____

8. Comment on the author's style of writing.

   Answer: When I read this passage, I feel _____

   _____

9. What have you learned?

   Answer: I have learned _____

   _____

10. During your reading of the text, what appeals to you that you'd like to try in your own writing?

    Answer: In my next writing I will try _____

   _____

Writing a Summary

Summarize the text in one paragraph, including (1) the title, author of the reading as well as the thesis statement; (2) significant details that support the main idea; and (3) restatement of the main idea in your own words. Note that the purpose of writing a summary is to accurately represent what the author wanted to say, not to provide a critique.

_____

_____

_____

_____

_____

_____

_____

_____

APPLICATION

Internet Activity

What does the DMV in New York claim about the usage of cellular devices for pedestrians? Can you find an argument for or against it? Post your findings on e-portfolios.

_____

_____

_____

_____

Reading-response Journal

Why do you feel that many people use iPods and games?

_____

_____

_____

_____

_____

_____

_____

_____

_____

Building Critical Thinking

Using a five-paragraph essay consisting of an introductory paragraph, three body paragraphs, and one concluding paragraph, state three reasons why you would either support or oppose legislation to fine those who use electronic devices while crossing city streets.

Prior to writing your essay, complete the outline in the back of this chapter by stating three arguments for and three arguments against the legislation. Once you have selected a position, complete the essay.

Upon completing your essay, tear out a *Peer Feedback Form* in the back of the chapter, exchange your essay with someone in the group, and review his or her essay by providing constructive comments. Return the essay to your classmate.

GRAMMAR PRACTICE VIA INTERNET

Go to one of the following websites:

- http://www.englishclub.com/grammar/conjunctions.htm

- http://www.towson.edu/ows/conjunctions.htm

Research conjunctions and write their definitions. Identify sentences that contain conjunctions from the reading and explain their structures on the lines below.

_____

_____

_____

_____

_____

_____

_____

THE OUTLINE

. . . .

I. Introduction

Thesis Statement – Main idea of your essay

_____

_____

II. First Body Paragraph – First topic sentence to support your thesis statement

_____

_____

Elaborate on your topic sentence

_____

Provide an example/evidence/quotation

_____

Explain the significance of the example/evidence/quotation

_____

III. Second Body Paragraph – Second topic sentence to support your thesis statement

_____

_____

Elaborate on your topic sentence

_____

Provide an example/evidence/quotation

_____

Explain the significance of the example/evidence/quotation

_____

IV. Third Body Paragraph – Third topic sentence to support your thesis statement

_____

_____

Elaborate on your topic sentence

_____

Provide an example/evidence/quotation

_____

Explain the significance of the example/evidence/quotation

_____

V. Conclusion

Summarize your topic sentences. Discuss how the ideas in your three body paragraphs support your thesis statement.

_____

_____

_____

Peer Feedback Form

Written by: _____

Feedback by: _____

Date: _____

Title of the Essay: _____

1. What is the main point of this paper?

    _____

    _____

    _____

2. What are the supporting details of this paper?

    _____

    _____

    _____

3. What is an interesting or unique feature of this paper?

    _____

    _____

    _____

4. How could the writer improve this paper when he or she rewrites it? Make at least one suggestion.

    _____

    _____

    _____

chapter 12
YOU'RE BEING WATCHED

PREREADING

Class Discussion

Discuss the following questions in a group.

1. Do you know if you have surveillance cameras near your house? Where are they?

   _____

   _____

   _____

2. What do the pictures on the next page remind you of?

   _____

   _____

   _____

3. Predict what the text will be about by reading the title.

   _____

   _____

   _____

Image courtesy of the author.

Image courtesy of the author.

ATTENTION!

As you enter this building, you are warned that you may be video/audio taped by as many as 37 or more surveillance cameras.

This sign in a midtown office tower whimsically makes the point that cameras are watching you wherever you go.

4. Predict what the text will be about by reading the first and last paragraphs (See pages 225-226).

_____

_____

5. Write how the author would develop the story.

_____

_____

Vocabulary in Context

Each item below includes a sentence from the reading. Using the context clues from this sentence, (1) determine the part of speech, and (2) formulate your own definition for the underlined word. Then (3) locate the word in a dictionary and write the appropriate definition.

1. "You don't even know if there's a tape in there. It's <u>creepy</u>." (Paragraph 4)

   (1) _____

   (2) _____

   (3)_____

2. "Another 292 cameras were <u>spotted</u> along 125th Street in central Harlem." (7)

   (1) _____

   (2) _____

   (3)_____

3. "There's no definitive count of cameras in the city, though they are concentrated in busy commercial <u>districts</u> and areas considered sensitive terror targets." (9)

   (1) _____

   (2)_____

   (3)_____

4. "A single camera in the elevator of a Crown Heights apartment building helped catch a suspect in the brutal <u>mugging</u> of an elderly woman this week." (10)

(1) _____

(2)_____

(3)_____

5. "That's where their <u>liability</u> is. Who's to say these guys aren't just watching pretty girls?" (12)

(1) _____

(2)_____

(3)_____

6. "The NYPD's recently released plan to install some 3,000 additional cameras raised concern at the NYCLU because it takes a new step in surveillance by creating a <u>data-base</u> of license plates and people's movements." (13)

(1) _____

(2)_____

(3)_____

READING

. . . .

YOU'RE BEING WATCHED

—Matthew Sweeney and Mariene Naanes

Cameras are everywhere in New York

[1]   They're everywhere and they're watching.

[2]   New York has become Camera City as our every coming and going is recorded.

[3]   Dropping off at the dry cleaners? Getting a cup of coffee at Starbucks? Crossing the street? Smile. For better or worse, you're on someone's security camera, whether it's the city's shopkeepers' or some nutjob's. A single busy block in Manhattan can contain hundreds.

[4]   "You don't know who's watching you," said Nicole Labruto, 24, of Woodside, Queens. "You don't even know if there's a tape in there. It's creepy."

[5]   For other New Yorkers, it's added security.

[6]   "Unless you're doing something wrong, you shouldn't worry," said Tracy Sugalski, 28, who lives near Union Square, "It sounds like a lot, but in New York City, aren't we always being watched?"

[7]   In 2005, the NYCLU counted more than 4,000 street-level cameras from the West Village down to Battery Park. Another 292 cameras were spotted along 125th Street in central Harlem.

[8]   "I would believe the number has dramatically increased" three years later," said Matt Faiella, staff attorney for the NYCLU.

[9]   There's no definitive count of cameras in the city, though they are concentrated in busy commercial districts and areas considered sensitive terror targets.

[10]   The cameras have myriad uses. The NYPD wants to install thousands to protect the city against terrorism. A single camera in the elevator of a Crown

Heights apartment building helped catch a suspect in the brutal mugging of an elderly woman this week. And on Wednesday Long Island police arrested a magician for secretly filming a mother and her two young daughters as they undressed in a changing room at his home office.

[11]   For security and surveillance experts, the real question about privacy starts after the images are taken.

[12]   "I go into hotels all the time; I see digital video recorders with [DVD] burners in there," said Desmond Smyth, president of Secur Watch 24, a Manhattan-based security company with some 11,000 cameras. "It's just amazing to me. That's where their liability is. Who's to say these guys aren't just watching pretty girls?"

[13]   The NYPD's recently released plan to install some 3,000 additional cameras raised concern at the NYCLU because it takes a new step in surveillance by creating a database of license plates and people's movements.

[14]   The police said the images, including license plate captures, would be erased after 30 days.

[15]   "Living in a surveillance society is a big change for most New Yorkers," Faiella said.

Poll: Do all the security cameras make you paranoid?

Surveillance Square
170 surveillance cameras were counted in one square block in Union Square, New York City. Here's a breakdown.
- Shoe Mania had the best hidden small cameras hanging on the ceiling
- L train subway station: 3
- Basic Plus, a small hardware and locksmith business, had four cameras
- Outdoors: 9
- Filene's Basement, the store with the most: 54

THE READING PROCESS

Topics, Main Ideas, and Details

1. What is the topic, or subject of this reading? Use the fewest words possible.

   _____

2. What is the main idea of this text? Underline it if directly stated. Write it in your own words if implied.

   _____

   _____

3. How is the main idea supported in the passage?

   _____

   _____

Identifying Details

Answer the following questions in complete sentences.

1. What store has the most cameras in Union Square?

   _____

   _____

2. What are some of the concerns about the constant surveillance?

   _____

   _____

   _____

3. How many cameras were in the area of the West Village to Battery Park in 2005?

_____

_____

4. How many cameras are along 125th Street in central Harlem?

_____

_____

5. What does the NYPD plan to do with surveillance cameras?

_____

_____

6. What does SecureWatch 24 do and how many cameras do they have?

_____

_____

_____

Open-ended Questions

1. Do you believe surveillance cameras have gone too far?

_____

_____

_____

2. What do you believe is the purpose of surveillance cameras in New York City?

_____

_____

_____

Drawing Inferences

The following information is not directly stated in the reading. Indicate whether the statement is true or false by writing T or F in the spaces provided.

_____ 1. Surveillance cameras are used only for photographs.

_____ 2. It is illegal to use a camera with a DVD burner in a hotel.

_____ 3. The NYPD uses cameras to assist in crime-watching.

_____ 4. Using cameras aids the city parking tickets and traffic violations revenues.

Useful Words/Phrases

1. In Paragraph 9, how would you use *definitive*? Use it in a sentence.

   _____

   _____

2. What is *paranoid*? Describe two symptoms of paranoia.

   _____

   _____

Idiomatic Expressions

1. In Paragraph 2, what is *every coming and going*?

   _____

   _____

2. In Paragraph 3, what is *for better or worse*? Have you even heard this phrase used in another place?

_____

_____

Vocabulary Practice

Match the underlined words with their definitions in the box. Write the appropriate answer letter in the spaces provided.

_____ 1. That <u>nutjob</u> almost ran me over!

_____ 2. We have a <u>breakdown</u> of the information, so we can properly answer the questions.

_____ 3. The sign <u>whimsically</u> noted that trespassers will be punished.

_____ 4. The constant <u>surveillance</u> gets unnerving after a while.

_____ 5. There are <u>numerous</u> ways to deal with a bully.

_____ 6. The number of casualties <u>dramatically</u> increased with the drop in supplies.

_____ 7. There is a <u>myriad</u> of stores to choose from in the mall.

a. crazy person

b. watch that is kept over a person or group

c. done oddly or fancifully

d. an analysis or classification of something

e. many

f. greatly or exponentially

g. group; selection

POSTREADING

Reading Strategies

Read the questions below and answer in the spaces provided.

1. In reading this passage, what are you reminded of?

   Answer: This reading reminds me of _____

   _____

2. Were you satisfied with your prereading prediction about the text?

   Answer: I was/wasn't satisfied because _____

   _____

3. Do you have any questions about the reading?

   Answer: I wonder _____

   _____

4. What did you visualize while reading this passage?

   Answer: I visualized _____

   _____

5. Is this passage making sense to you?

   Answer: This passage is/isn't making sense to me because _____

   _____

6. What is the main idea of this reading?

   Answer: This reading is about _____

   _____

7. How can you relate the main idea to your own experiences?

Answer: I can relate this passage to _____

_____

8. Comment on the author's style of writing.

Answer: When I read this passage, I feel _____

_____

9. What have you learned?

Answer: I have learned _____

_____

10. During your reading of the text, what appeals to you that you'd like to try in your own writing?

Answer: In my next writing I will try _____

_____

Writing a Summary

Summarize the text in one paragraph, including (1) the title, author of the reading as well as the thesis statement; (2) significant details that support the main idea; and (3) restatement of the main idea in your own words. Note that the purpose of writing a summary is to accurately represent what the author wanted to say, not to provide a critique.

_____

_____

_____

_____

_____

_____

_____

_____

APPLICATION

Internet Activities

1. Find out if it is legal to film people without their permission.

   _____

   _____

   _____

2. Go to the homeland security website and find three purposes for this government agency.

_____

_____

_____

Reading-response Journal

Do surveillance cameras improve people's behavior? Do they make you think twice about your actions?

_____

_____

_____

_____

_____

_____

_____

_____

_____

_____

Building Critical Thinking

Using a five-paragraph essay consisting of an introductory paragraph, three body paragraphs, and one concluding paragraph, state three reasons why you would either support or oppose surveillance cameras in the city.

Prior to writing your essay, complete the outline in the back of the chapter by stating three arguments for and three arguments against surveillance cameras in New York City. Once you have selected a position, complete the essay.

Upon completing your essay, tear out a *Peer Feedback Form* in the back of the chapter, exchange your essay with someone in the group, and review his or her essay by providing constructive comments. Return the essay to your classmate.

GRAMMAR PRACTICE VIA INTERNET

Go to one of the following websites:

- http://www.englishpage.com/modals/modalintro.html

- http://www.learnenglish.de/grammar/verbmodal.htm

Research modal verbs and write their definitions. Identify sentences that contain modal verbs from the reading and explain their structures on the lines below.

_____

_____

_____

_____

_____

_____

_____

_____

_____

_____

THE OUTLINE
. . . .

I. Introduction

Thesis Statement – Main idea of your essay

_____

_____

II. First Body Paragraph – First topic sentence to support your thesis statement

_____

_____

Elaborate on your topic sentence

_____

Provide an example/evidence/quotation

_____

Explain the significance of the example/evidence/quotation

_____

III. Second Body Paragraph – Second topic sentence to support your thesis statement

_____

_____

Elaborate on your topic sentence

_____

Provide an example/evidence/quotation

_____

Explain the significance of the example/evidence/quotation

_____

IV. Third Body Paragraph – Third topic sentence to support your thesis statement

_____

_____

Elaborate on your topic sentence

_____

Provide an example/evidence/quotation

_____

Explain the significance of the example/evidence/quotation

_____

V. Conclusion

Summarize your topic sentences. Discuss how the ideas in your three body paragraphs support your thesis statement.

_____

_____

_____

Peer Feedback Form

Written by: _____

Feedback by: _____

Date: _____

Title of the Essay: _____

1. What is the main point of this paper?

   _____

   _____

   _____

2. What are the supporting details of this paper?

   _____

   _____

   _____

3. What is an interesting or unique feature of this paper?

   _____

   _____

   _____

4. How could the writer improve this paper when he or she rewrites it? Make at least one suggestion.

   _____

   _____

   _____

Image © Isaphia, 2012. Shutterstock, Inc.

unit 7
MOVING FORWARD

chapter 13

MAKING WAVES AT THE SEAPORT

PREREADING

Class Discussion

Discuss the following questions in a group.

1. Do you like high-rise buildings? Explain why or why not.

   _____

   _____

   _____

2. What do the pictures on the next page remind you of?

   _____

   _____

   _____

3. Predict what the text will be about by reading the title.

   _____

   _____

   _____

Image © Steven Lee, 2012. Shutterstock, Inc.

Image © William A. Mueller (mere artist), 2012. Shutterstock, Inc.

Among the plans for South Street Seaport are mixed-use, high-rise buildings.

4. Predict what the text will be about by reading the first and last paragraphs (See pages 243-244).

_____

_____

5. Write how the author would develop the story.

_____

_____

Vocabulary in Context

Each item below includes a sentence from the reading. Using the context clues from this sentence, (1) determine the part of speech, and (2) formulate your own definition for the underlined word. Then (3) locate the word in a dictionary and write the appropriate definition.

1. "It needs to be <u>weaved</u> into New York City instead of being its isolated, insulated, little world." (Paragraph 4)

    (1) _____

    (2) _____

    (3) _____

2. "It's a neighborhood undergoing an <u>immense</u> amount of change, and there are a lot of interesting ideas about how to fill the void." (4)

    (1) _____

    (2) _____

    (3) _____

3. "The seaport needs to evolve and be <u>re-knitted</u> back into the life of the city while preserving its history." (7)

(1) _____

(2) _____

(3) _____

4. "The seaport needs to evolve and be re-knitted back into the life of the city while <u>preserving</u> its history." (7)

(1) _____

(2) _____

(3) _____

5. "This is really New York's last opportunity to preserve our historic, <u>nautical</u>, seafaring roots." (8)

(1) _____

(2) _____

(3) _____

6. "This is really New York's last opportunity to preserve our historic, nautical, <u>seafaring</u> roots." (8)

(1) _____

(2) _____

(3) _____

READING

MAKING WAVES AT THE SEAPORT

—David Freedlander

Most agree makeover needed

[1]   The South Street Seaport, an area for decades dismissed as "just for tourists," has re-emerged in the forefront of New Yorkers' minds as architects, preservationists and local residents wrestle over the waterfront of the future.

[2]   It's been two years since the old salts who hawked their wares at the Fulton Fish Market packed up their ice and grime and decamped for the cleaner climes of the Bronx, clearing the way for the neighborhood's transformation.

[3]   What the feel of the new Seaport will be is still unknown.

[4]   "It needs to be weaved into New York City instead of being its isolated, insulated, little world," said Simeon Bankoff of the Historic District Council. "It's a neighborhood undergoing an immense amount of change, and there are a lot of interesting ideas about how to fill the void."

[5]   Plans are moving forward quickly. Already in the works is the development of several new high-rise buildings that would allow for both residential and commercial uses.

[6]   "I've lived in the area for over 20 years, and 90 percent of the change has happened in the last two years," said Gary Fagin, a neighborhood activist. "You'll forgive the metaphor, but it's been a sea change."

[7]   Most agree that the Seaport needs to evolve and be re-knitted back into the life of the city while preserving its history, but there is broad disagreement on how to do that.

[8]   "This is really New York's last opportunity to preserve our historic, nautical, seafaring roots," said Councilman Alan Gerson (D-Manhattan), who represents the area.

[9]   Already many 19th century buildings have faced the developer's wrecking ball, most notably 213 Pearl St., New York's original World Trade Center, which is being replaced by a hotel.

[10]   "I know the urge to build and make money out of a piece of real estate is primal in New York, but I think we should save more of the old things," said Jack Putnam, a historian at the South Street Seaport Museum.

A Rich History
Changing uses of the Seaport
Transformation of the Seaport
- 1815-1860: The Seaport's heyday as a maritime port
- 1880-1930: Area slowly declines as ships use west side and New Jersey piers
- 1966: Community group Friends of South Street Maritime Museum rallies to preserve area from condemnation and abandonment
- 1979: Rouse Company begins redevelopment of area as "Festival Marketplace"
- 2007: Plans floated to demolish mall and reconstruct high-rise towers
(Source: Encyclopedia of NYC, amNY)

Study Notes: Literary Terms

The title of the article employs a literary term, imagery. Explore how the following terms can be used differently.

INSPIRATION

- simile – a direct comparison between two things that are different, using *like* or *as*. e.g., Your eyes shine like the stars.

- metaphor – an indirect comparison between two things that are different, saying one thing *is* another. e.g., Your eyes are stars.

- imagery – the descriptive words an author uses to help readers see, hear, smell, taste, or touch what is being described. e.g., The sky had gold and orange stripes below the clouds.

THE READING PROCESS
· ·

Topics, Main Ideas, and Details

1. What is the topic, or subject of this reading? Use the fewest words possible.

     _____

2. What is the main idea of this text? Underline it if directly stated. Write it in your own words if implied.

     _____

     _____

3. How is the main idea supported in the passage?

     _____

     _____

Identifying Details

Answer the following questions in complete sentences.

1. What was the original function of South Street Seaport?

     _____

     _____

2. How was South Street Seaport seen to many people?

     _____

     _____

3. Who struggled to have control over the Seaport's future?

     _____

     _____

4. What plans were already in development at the time of this article?

_____

_____

5. When has the most change occurred for the Seaport?

_____

_____

6. What time period was the Seaport's heyday?

_____

_____

7. Why did the Seaport area begin to decline?

_____

_____

Open-ended Questions

Answer the following questions in complete sentences.

1. What is so appealing about South Seaport to New Yorkers?

_____

_____

2. What do you think is the future of South Seaport?

_____

_____

CHAPTER 13: Making Waves at the Seaport

Drawing Inferences

The following information is not directly stated in the reading. Infer what the author would say is true. Indicate whether the statement is true or false by writing T or F in the spaces provided.

_____ 1. The South Seaport area is dedicated only to New York tourism.

_____ 2. Some New Yorkers like to merge old architecture with new.

_____ 3. The neighborhoods and historians agree on converting the Seaport into high-rise apartments.

_____ 4. The Seaport has undergone many different changes from 2005 to 2007.

Useful Words/Phrases

1. In Paragraph 4, what is the meaning of *fill the void*?

   _____

   _____

2. In Paragraph 9, what is the meaning of *wrecking ball*?

   _____

   _____

Idiomatic Expressions

1. In Paragraph 3, what is the meaning of *the feel of*?

   _____

   _____

2. In Paragraph 4, what is the meaning of *little world*?

_____

_____

Vocabulary Practice

Fill-in-the-Blanks

Choose one of the following words to best complete the sentences below. Some of the words were modified. Use each word only once. Be sure to pay close attention to the context clues provided.

dismissed	forefront	preservation

1. The idea was immediately _____ once they realized how foolish it was.

2. We began the _____ of the city's historical buildings.

3. Texas was at the _____ of the battles that took place during the war.

salts	wrestle	hawk

4. After the thief got away with the stolen goods, he began to _____ them anyway he could.

5. We continued to _____ for control over the party.

6. The old _____ always told stories of their days at sea.

wares	decamped	grime

7. The _____ was embedded into the wall so it was hard to get out.

8. Her _____ were shoddy and poorly made.

9. Once he got his court summons, he quickly _____ for Cuba.

weave	clime	insulated

10. This _____ is rather dull and boring.

11. We began to _____ a plan with the information we were given.

12. This region is very well _____ from the other countries.

undergo	void	metaphors

13. Poetry is full of _____ that give the reader a better visualization of the author's message.

14. The machine had to _____ many repairs.

15. She constantly tried to fill that _____ in her heart by chasing small pleasures.

re-knit	seafaring	wreck

16. A sailor's _____ life is usually all he knows.

17. The crew began to _____ the old building to make way for the new hotel.

18. After her near death experience, she tried to _____ her relationship with all of her friends and family.

urge	primal	heyday

19. When angered, Bob becomes consumed by _____ rage.

20. In his _____ it is said that he was a very handsome man.

21. I _____ you to reconsider your decision.

maritime	rally	condemnation

22. Her _____ mansion had a perfect view of the ocean.

23. The _____ of his acts caused him to quit.

24. The _____ was called in order to motivate the citizens and boost morale.

float	abandonment

25. The _____ of his post demoralized the whole force.

26. The idea continued to _____ in our minds even after we tried to dismiss it.

POSTREADING

Reading Strategies

Read the questions below and answer in the spaces provided.

1. In reading this passage, what are you reminded of?

   Answer: This reading reminds me of _____

   _____

2. Were you satisfied with your prereading prediction about the text?

   Answer: I was/wasn't satisfied because _____

   _____

3. Do you have any questions about the reading?

   Answer: I wonder _____

   _____

4. What did you visualize while reading this passage?

   Answer: I visualized _____

   _____

5. Is this passage making sense to you?

   Answer: This passage is/isn't making sense to me because _____

   _____

6. What is the main idea of this reading?

   Answer: This reading is about _____

   _____

7. How can you relate the main idea to your own experiences?

   Answer: I can relate this passage to _____

   _____

8. Comment on the author's style of writing.

   Answer: When I read this passage, I feel _____

   _____

9. What have you learned?

   Answer: I have learned _____

   _____

10. During your reading of the text, what appeals to you that you'd like to try in your own writing?

    Answer: In my next writing I will try _____

    _____

Writing a Summary

Summarize the text in one paragraph, including (1) the title, author of the reading as well as the thesis statement; (2) significant details that support the main idea; and (3) restatement of the main idea in your own words. Note that the purpose of writing a summary is to accurately represent what the author wanted to say, not to provide a critique.

_____

_____

_____

_____

_____

_____

_____

_____

_____

APPLICATION

Internet Activity

Look up the background history of the South Street Seaport. Select three time periods laid out in the reading and discuss changes of each period.

_____

_____

_____

_____

_____

Reading-response Journal

Discuss your feelings about urban renewal. What happens to the people when a community is refurbished?

_____

_____

_____

_____

_____

_____

_____

_____

Building Critical Thinking

Using a five-paragraph essay consisting of an introductory paragraph, three body paragraphs, and one concluding paragraph, make an argument that would either support or oppose building high rise condominiums/apartments in the South Seaport area. Explain how your choice would best serve the interests of the people of New York City.

Prior to writing your essay, complete the outline in the back of the chapter and then complete the essay.

Upon completing your essay, tear out a *Peer Feedback Form* in the back of the chapter, exchange your essay with someone in the group, and review his or her essay by providing constructive comments. Return the essay to your classmate.

GRAMMAR PRACTICE VIA INTERNET

Go to one of the following websites:

- http://www.chompchomp.com/terms/clause.htm

- http://www.towson.edu/ows/sentelmt.htm

- http://web.cn.edu/kwheeler/gram_clauses_n_phrases.html

Research what *clauses* are and write their definitions. Use information to refer back to reading for sentence structure containing *dependent* and *independent clauses*. Write down two sentences on the lines below. Underline the *dependent* clause and circle the *independent* clause.

_____

_____

_____

_____

_____

_____

THE OUTLINE

· ·

I. Introduction

Thesis Statement – Main idea of your essay

_____

_____

II. First Body Paragraph – First topic sentence to support your thesis statement

_____

_____

Elaborate on your topic sentence

_____

Provide an example/evidence/quotation

_____

Explain the significance of the example/evidence/quotation

_____

III. Second Body Paragraph – Second topic sentence to support your thesis statement

_____

_____

Elaborate on your topic sentence

_____

Provide an example/evidence/quotation

_____

Explain the significance of the example/evidence/quotation

_____

IV. Third Body Paragraph – Third topic sentence to support your thesis statement

_____

_____

Elaborate on your topic sentence

_____

Provide an example/evidence/quotation

_____

Explain the significance of the example/evidence/quotation

_____

V. Conclusion

Summarize your topic sentences. Discuss how the ideas in your three body paragraphs support your thesis statement.

_____

_____

_____

Peer Feedback Form

Written by: _____

Feedback by: _____

Date: _____

Title of the Essay: _____

1. What is the main point of this paper?

   _____

   _____

   _____

2. What are the supporting details of this paper?

   _____

   _____

   _____

3. What is an interesting or unique feature of this paper?

   _____

   _____

   _____

4. How could the writer improve this paper when he or she rewrites it? Make at least one suggestion.

   _____

   _____

   _____

chapter 14

AFTER 20 YEARS, IS THE WEBSITE ABOUT TO BECOME EXTINCT?

PREREADING
. . . .

Class Discussion

Discuss the following questions in a group.

1. How many hours a day approximately do you spend on the Internet?

   _____

   _____

   _____

2. What do the pictures on the next page remind you of?

   _____

   _____

   _____

3. Predict what the text will be about by reading the title.

   _____

   _____

   _____

Image © Tumanyan, 2012. Shutterstock, Inc.

Image courtesy of the author.

CHAPTER 14: After 20 Years, Is the Website about to Become Extinct?

4. Predict what the text will be about by reading the first and last paragraphs.

_____

_____

5. Write how the author would develop the story.

_____

_____

Vocabulary in Context

Each item below includes a sentence from the reading. Using the context clues from this sentence, (1) determine the part of speech, and (2) formulate your own definition for the underlined word/phrase. Then (3) locate the word in a dictionary and write the appropriate definition.

1. "It <u>charts</u> the evolution of websites and web design over the past 20 years." (Paragraph 1)

   (1) _____

   (2) _____

   (3) _____

2. "We discussed how web design <u>trends</u> have evolved over the years, along with the difficulties of archiving increasingly interactive and social content on modern websites." (2)

   (1) _____

   (2) _____

   (3) _____

3. "We discussed how web design trends have evolved over the years, <u>along with</u> the difficulties of archiving increasingly interactive and social content on modern websites." (2)

   (1) _____

   (2) _____

   (3) _____

4. "Looking back on websites from the mid-1990s, you can clearly see the evolutionary link to many of the sites and apps from this <u>era</u>." (3)

(1) _____

(2)_____

(3)_____

5. "The very first website, a historical moment in time, has been lost forever," <u>lamented</u> Boulton." (5)

(1) _____

(2)_____

(3)_____

6. "Grotke's team <u>collaborates</u> closely with the Internet Archive, the non-profit site that runs the Wayback Machine." (7)

(1) _____

(2)_____

(3)_____

7. "So whereas websites are 'destinations that you go to to find information,' according to Boulton, the current era is increasingly about information coming to the individual and interacting with it on devices like smartphones." (10)

(1) _____

(2)_____

(3)_____

READING

AFTER 20 YEARS, IS THE WEBSITE ABOUT TO BECOME EXTINCT?

—Richard Macmanus

In this chapter, you need to go online to read the passage entitled, *"After 20 Years, Is The Website About to Become Extinct?"* **at**

http://www.readwriteweb.com/archives/is_the_website_about_to_become_ extinct.php

THE READING PROCESS

Topics, Main Ideas, and Details

1. What is the topic, or subject of this reading? Use the fewest words possible.

   _____

2. What is the main idea of this text? Underline it if directly stated. Write it in your own words if implied.

   _____

   _____

3. How is the main idea supported in the passage?

   _____

   _____

Identifying Details

Answer the following questions in complete sentences.

1. Who was the Curator of the Digital Archaeology exhibit?

   _____

   _____

   _____

2. What was the first website ever made? Who made it?

   _____

   _____

   _____

3. What site was said to be one of the first animated websites?

   _____

   _____

   _____

4. What site was an ancestor of the iPad app Flipboard?

   _____

   _____

   _____

5. Why can't Grotke's Web Archiving Team archive modern websites?

   _____

   _____

   _____

6. What does Boulton think will happen to websites?

_____

_____

_____

Open-ended Questions

1. Who is the keeper of your memories in your family?

_____

_____

_____

2. What kind of books do you have a collection of?

_____

_____

_____

Drawing Inferences

The following information is not directly stated in the reading. Indicate whether the statement is true or false by writing T or F in the spaces provided.

_____ 1. Websites and their design have remained stable over the past years.

_____ 2. Due to technological advancement, animation on websites has been improved.

_____ 3. An older version of iPad app Flipboard is e/zineword.com

_____ 4. With the genesis of the social web, more people are developing social skills.

Useful Words/Phrases

1. In Paragraph 1, what does it mean by *highlights of*?

    _____

    _____

2. What is the meaning of *evolutionary link*?

    _____

    _____

Idiomatic Expressions

1. In Paragraph 4, what is *the voice of the people*?

    _____

    _____

2. In Paragraph 5, what is the meaning of *moment in time*?

    _____

    _____

Vocabulary Practice

Fill-in-the-Blanks

Choose one of the following words to best complete the sentences below. Some of the words were modified. Use each word only once. Be sure to pay close attention to the context clues provided.

chart	exhibit	archived

1. The _____ on American history was laid out very well.

2. She _____ the information so she could find it again easily.

3. He began to _____ the history of technology for his science project.

apps	extinct	archaeology

4. Many who study _____ have to be very well versed in history.

5. That particular red gazelle became _____ after years of over hunting.

6. The iPhone has access to thousands of _____.

pixilated	bypassed	curator

7. The _____ of the museum took regular walks around to look at the displays.

8. The screen was so _____ that I could hardly see the video.

9. He _____ his firewall and that caused him to get a computer virus.

era	transient	screenshots

10. Many movies often release _____ to further entice the viewers.

11. During the _____ of the Iraq War, many people were misled when it came to the reason for the war.

12. The joy she felt was _____.

sums up	collaborate	crawlable

13. We decided to _____ in order to complete the project in time.

14. A conclusion sentence often _____ the paragraph.

15. Modern day websites are not _____ like some of the first websites created.

static	disposable

16. Most people use _____ paper towels as opposed to cloth towels.

17. An object will stay _____ till an outside force causes it to move.

POSTREADING
· ·

Reading Strategies

Read the questions below and answer in the spaces provided.

1. In reading this passage, what are you reminded of?

    Answer: This reading reminds me of _____

    _____

2. Were you satisfied with your prereading prediction about the text?

    Answer: I was/wasn't satisfied because_____

    _____

3. Do you have any questions about the reading?

    Answer: I wonder _____

    _____

4. What did you visualize while reading this passage?

    Answer: I visualized _____

    _____

5. Is this passage making sense to you?

    Answer: This passage is/isn't making sense to me because _____

    _____

6. What is the main idea of this reading?

    Answer: This reading is about _____

    _____

7. How can you relate the main idea to your own experiences?

   Answer: I can relate this passage to _____

   _____

8. Comment on the author's style of writing.

   Answer: When I read this passage, I feel _____

   _____

9. What have you learned?

   Answer: I have learned _____

   _____

10. During your reading of the text, what appeals to you that you'd like to try in your own writing?

    Answer: In my next writing I will try_____

    _____

Writing a Summary

Summarize the text in one paragraph, including (1) the title, author of the reading as well as the thesis statement; (2) significant details that support the main idea; and (3) restatement of the main idea in your own words. Note that the purpose of writing a summary is to accurately represent what the author wanted to say, not to provide a critique.

_____

_____

_____

_____

_____

_____

APPLICATION

Internet Activities

1. Look up ReadWriteWeb.com. What is it?

   _____

   _____

   _____

   _____

2. Look up Waybackmachine.com. Go to the news section and choose an article to write two sentences about.

   _____

   _____

   _____

   _____

Reading-response Journal

Why do you think it is necessary to keep a collection of websites? What purpose do they serve?

_____

_____

_____

_____

_____

Building Critical Thinking

Using a five-paragraph essay consisting of an introductory paragraph, three body paragraphs, and one concluding paragraph, write an essay based on the following question.

What legacy do you want to leave for your posterity?

Prior to writing your essay, complete the outline in the back of this chapter and then complete the essay.

Upon completing your essay, tear out a *Peer Feedback Form* in the back of the chapter, exchange your essay with someone in the group, and review his or her essay by providing constructive comments. Return the essay to your classmate.

GRAMMAR PRACTICE VIA INTERNET

Go to one of the following websites:

- http://www.learnenglish.de/grammar/articlestext.htm

- http://www.eslbase.com/grammar/articles

Research articles – definite and indefinite and write their definitions. Identify two sentences that contain articles from the reading and explain their structures on the lines below.

_____

_____

_____

_____

_____

_____

_____

THE OUTLINE

I. Introduction

Thesis Statement – Main idea of your essay

_____

_____

II. First Body Paragraph – First topic sentence to support your thesis statement

_____

_____

Elaborate on your topic sentence

_____

Provide an example/evidence/quotation

_____

Explain the significance of the example/evidence/quotation

_____

III. Second Body Paragraph – Second topic sentence to support your thesis statement

_____

_____

Elaborate on your topic sentence

_____

Provide an example/evidence/quotation

_____

Explain the significance of the example/evidence/quotation

_____

IV. Third Body Paragraph – Third topic sentence to support your thesis statement

_____

_____

Elaborate on your topic sentence

_____

Provide an example/evidence/quotation

_____

Explain the significance of the example/evidence/quotation

_____

V. Conclusion

Summarize your topic sentences. Discuss how the ideas in your three body paragraphs support your thesis statement.

_____

_____

_____

THE OUTLINE

I. Introduction

Thesis Statement – Main idea of your essay

_____

_____

II. First Body Paragraph – First topic sentence to support your thesis statement

_____

_____

Elaborate on your topic sentence

_____

Provide an example/evidence/quotation

_____

Explain the significance of the example/evidence/quotation

_____

III. Second Body Paragraph – Second topic sentence to support your thesis statement

_____

_____

Elaborate on your topic sentence

_____

Provide an example/evidence/quotation

_____

Explain the significance of the example/evidence/quotation

_____

IV. Third Body Paragraph – Third topic sentence to support your thesis statement

_____

_____

Elaborate on your topic sentence

_____

Provide an example/evidence/quotation

_____

Explain the significance of the example/evidence/quotation

_____

V. Conclusion

Summarize your topic sentences. Discuss how the ideas in your three body paragraphs support your thesis statement.

_____

_____

_____

THE OUTLINE

I. Introduction

Thesis Statement – Main idea of your essay

_____

_____

II. First Body Paragraph – First topic sentence to support your thesis statement

_____

_____

Elaborate on your topic sentence

_____

Provide an example/evidence/quotation

_____

Explain the significance of the example/evidence/quotation

_____

III. Second Body Paragraph – Second topic sentence to support your thesis statement

_____

_____

Elaborate on your topic sentence

_____

Provide an example/evidence/quotation

_____

Explain the significance of the example/evidence/quotation

_____

IV. Third Body Paragraph – Third topic sentence to support your thesis statement

_____

_____

Elaborate on your topic sentence

_____

Provide an example/evidence/quotation

_____

Explain the significance of the example/evidence/quotation

_____

V. Conclusion

Summarize your topic sentences. Discuss how the ideas in your three body paragraphs support your thesis statement.

_____

_____

_____

THE OUTLINE

I. Introduction

Thesis Statement – Main idea of your essay

_____

_____

II. First Body Paragraph – First topic sentence to support your thesis statement

_____

_____

Elaborate on your topic sentence

_____

Provide an example/evidence/quotation

_____

Explain the significance of the example/evidence/quotation

_____

III. Second Body Paragraph – Second topic sentence to support your thesis statement

_____

_____

Elaborate on your topic sentence

_____

Provide an example/evidence/quotation

_____

Explain the significance of the example/evidence/quotation

_____

IV. Third Body Paragraph – Third topic sentence to support your thesis statement

_____

_____

Elaborate on your topic sentence

_____

Provide an example/evidence/quotation

_____

Explain the significance of the example/evidence/quotation

_____

V. Conclusion

Summarize your topic sentences. Discuss how the ideas in your three body paragraphs support your thesis statement.

_____

_____

_____

THE OUTLINE
. . . .

I. Introduction

Thesis Statement – Main idea of your essay

_____

_____

II. First Body Paragraph – First topic sentence to support your thesis statement

_____

_____

Elaborate on your topic sentence

_____

Provide an example/evidence/quotation

_____

Explain the significance of the example/evidence/quotation

_____

III. Second Body Paragraph – Second topic sentence to support your thesis statement

_____

_____

Elaborate on your topic sentence

_____

Provide an example/evidence/quotation

_____

Explain the significance of the example/evidence/quotation

_____

IV. Third Body Paragraph – Third topic sentence to support your thesis statement

_____

_____

Elaborate on your topic sentence

_____

Provide an example/evidence/quotation

_____

Explain the significance of the example/evidence/quotation

_____

V. Conclusion

Summarize your topic sentences. Discuss how the ideas in your three body paragraphs support your thesis statement.

_____

_____

_____

Peer Feedback Form

Written by: _____

Feedback by: _____

Date: _____

Title of the Essay: _____

1. What is the main point of this paper?

   _____

   _____

   _____

2. What are the supporting details of this paper?

   _____

   _____

   _____

3. What is an interesting or unique feature of this paper?

   _____

   _____

   _____

4. How could the writer improve this paper when he or she rewrites it? Make at least one suggestion.

   _____

   _____

   _____

Peer Feedback Form

Written by: _____

Feedback by: _____

Date: _____

Title of the Essay: _____

1. What is the main point of this paper?

   _____

   _____

   _____

2. What are the supporting details of this paper?

   _____

   _____

   _____

3. What is an interesting or unique feature of this paper?

   _____

   _____

   _____

4. How could the writer improve this paper when he or she rewrites it? Make at least one suggestion.

   _____

   _____

   _____

Peer Feedback Form

Written by: _____

Feedback by: _____

Date: _____

Title of the Essay: _____

1. What is the main point of this paper?

   _____

   _____

   _____

2. What are the supporting details of this paper?

   _____

   _____

   _____

3. What is an interesting or unique feature of this paper?

   _____

   _____

   _____

4. How could the writer improve this paper when he or she rewrites it? Make at least one suggestion.

   _____

   _____

   _____

Peer Feedback Form

Written by: _____

Feedback by: _____

Date: _____

Title of the Essay: _____

1. What is the main point of this paper?

   _____

   _____

   _____

2. What are the supporting details of this paper?

   _____

   _____

   _____

3. What is an interesting or unique feature of this paper?

   _____

   _____

   _____

4. How could the writer improve this paper when he or she rewrites it? Make at least one suggestion.

   _____

   _____

   _____

Peer Feedback Form

Written by: _____

Feedback by: _____

Date: _____

Title of the Essay: _____

1. What is the main point of this paper?

   _____

   _____

   _____

2. What are the supporting details of this paper?

   _____

   _____

   _____

3. What is an interesting or unique feature of this paper?

   _____

   _____

   _____

4. How could the writer improve this paper when he or she rewrites it? Make at least one suggestion.

   _____

   _____

   _____